Is Organized Labor A Decaying Business Model?

Is Organized Labor A Decaying Business Model?

CHRIS MOSQUERA

Outskirts Press, Inc.
Denver, Colorado

The opinions expressed in this manuscript are solely the opinions of the author and do not represent the opinions or thoughts of the publisher. The author has represented and warranted full ownership and/or legal right to publish all the materials in this book.

Is Organized Labor A Decaying Business Model?
All Rights Reserved.
Copyright © 2009 Chris Mosquera
v3.0

Cover Photo © 2009 JupiterImages Corporation. All rights reserved - used with permission.

This book may not be reproduced, transmitted, or stored in whole or in part by any means, including graphic, electronic, or mechanical without the express written consent of the publisher except in the case of brief quotations embodied in critical articles and reviews.

Outskirts Press, Inc.
http://www.outskirtspress.com

ISBN: 978-1-4327-4586-8

Outskirts Press and the "OP" logo are trademarks belonging to Outskirts Press, Inc.

PRINTED IN THE UNITED STATES OF AMERICA

Abstract

Is Organized Labor A Decaying Business Model?

This book examines the organized labor business model from the perspectives of the economic and political influences of organized labor relative to the domestic and global economy. The traditional organized labor business model, as we have known it over the past century, is not sustainable in its present form, and will become less relevant, irrelevant or extinct, unless major changes are made. The nature of work has changed, and labor unions have failed to evolve with this change, just as dinosaurs became extinct because they failed to evolve with the climatic changes.

Union representation serves a very important business and economic function. Repressive employers create strong unions, because unions protect workers from abusive management. The organized labor business model for growth is to unionize low-wage workers, such as immigrants, minorities, and females, in industries and locations with traditionally low union saturation.

Historically, labor unions have encouraged an adversarial (*us* versus *them*) approach to business operations. The key to long-term survival, increased economic strength, and political power lies in the ability to adapt to changes, become productive allies with business, and be part of the solution, not part of the problem. To do less will result in a decayed organized labor business model creating its own irrelevance and going the way of the dinosaurs.

Executive Summary

Is Organized Labor a Decaying Business Model? The answer is not a definitive yes or no, but rather yes and no. If organized labor continues in the same manner it has for the last century, then the probability of relevant existence in the next century is very slim, and labor will become the one-century wonder. Unions must accept the new paradigm, which is the nature of work is changing, and will continue to evolve. The economic forces of globalization are a major contributor to this evolution, as is the shift towards an internet based information society. The traditional industrial and manufacturing blue-collar labor union business model is being replaced with robotics, technology, outsourcing, downsizing, and globalization. A prime example is the automotive industry.

Big labor is big business, but still stuck in the last century. Unions have failed to accept that the nature of work has changed. Business as usual, usually means that you are out of business. Market forces are forcing economic changes, and unless labor adapts quickly, it will become irrelevant in the global market. Virtually every product and most services can be performed offshore in low wage countries, or outsourced to lower wage states, using eager low-wage non-union workers.

The internet and technology, has created the global 24-hour workday. When it is night in the western hemisphere, it is day in the eastern hemisphere and workers can perform back office functions ready for the workers the next business day. Telephone communications is seamlessly transferring calls to worldwide call centers, where cheerful representatives, will answer your concerns in the language you have chosen. *"For English press one, for Spanish press two, and for other languages, please press three,"* is the globalized method for customer service communications.

American car companies can make cars in China, and sell them in Detroit, cheaper than making the cars in Detroit, and selling them in America. These same American car companies can make cars in China and sell them worldwide, even cheaper, and for a greater profit, than selling the same cars in the United States. To an extent, labor unions are to blame. They have priced labor above economic returns. This oversight is a significant contributor to the decline of the organized labor business model.

Labor, in its basic element, is a commodity, like any raw material or production facility. Best business practices mandates that companies go where they make the most profit. Labor is expensive. Corporate America has fought back, by outsourcing, moving to non-union and less expensive environments, downsizing, embracing technology, and by aggressively fighting union organizing campaigns. It is not personal, just business.

The survival business model for organized labor is to become more relevant with the times and re-format itself to meet the needs of its members. Corporate America uses a similar business model, as they shed old products, and old production methods. Corporate America emerges leaner and more agile, able to meet product demands quickly and adjust to market realities. Unions need to adjust their business model to market realities and become more business centric and less fraternal.

If organized labor is to survive, it must look to the past to see the future. Labor unions have become complacent, unable, or unwilling to adjust to change. The axiom of unions being *"male, pale, and stale"* has some merit. Unions are coming to the slow realization they must shed their old-boy ways, and embrace immigrants, minorities, service workers, and all disenfranchised workers. Traditional industrial blue-collar workers in heavy manufacturing are declining, and no company or industry wants to bet on a loosing horse. A case in point is the United Auto Workers Union (UAW).

Politically and economically, the future for organized labor as an industry is with the sectors of the economy that have been previously ignored. This includes service sector employment, low-wage workers, minorities, and immigrants. These workers need the services that unions provide, such as better wages and benefits, better health care, and collective bargaining benefits. Unions must return to their roots. Historically, unions represented oppressed workers, which is exactly the category that minorities, immigrants, and low-wage workers represent.

Unions have seen better days. Private sector unions have experienced a rapid decline in membership and industry saturation, as companies search for lower cost business models. Public sector unions are the only bright spot, and these numbers are barely holding steady as governments on all levels are facing the dilemma of servicing more people with shrinking budgets.

The key to union growth is organizing, and the mantra of "<u>Organize or Perish</u>" is an absolute. Organizing is the method for unions to grow and expand their business. Companies expand by adding paying clients. Unions expand by adding dues paying members. Corporate America wishes to remain non-union, and when faced with an organizing attempt, swings a heavy hammer spending vast sums to remain union free.

The labor relations business (*'union busting'* in the labor vernacular) is a huge industry on to itself, and has been a significant contributing factor to the decline of unions. The goals of the labor consultants are to convince employees that unions are bad, and the company is good. Companies that hire professional labor consultants, have a significantly higher win rate over those companies that try to do it in house, or do nothing at all.

Unions argue that labor laws are written to support the employer, and make organizing difficult. That will change when some version of the *"Employee Free Choice Act"* (EFCA), becomes the labor law of the land. It will simplify and speed labor's ability to unionize companies. Organized labor considers the EFCA vital to the survival of the labor movement, and has pledged to spend hundreds of millions of dollars on securing its passage. The Service Employees International Union believes the legislation would enable it to organize a million workers per year, up from its current pace of 100,000 workers per year.

Currently, companies can demand a secret-ballot election to determine union representation. Those elections often are preceded by months of aggressive employer anti union campaigns, and union and employee pro union campaigns. Under the proposed legislation, companies may no longer have the right to insist on a secret ballot. Instead, the Free Choice, or *"card check"*, legislation would let unions form if more than 50% of workers simply sign a card saying they want to join.

Unions thrive when employment relationships are oppressive and exploitative. Unions have difficulties organizing companies when employees are happy, fairly compensated, and productive. Simple stated, repressive employers create strong unions, and great employers do not have unions. Happy workers are productive workers, and all the stakeholders benefit.

Union labor has priced itself out of the global marketplace. Industrial employment is often outsourced to non-union low wage nations. Private industry must earn a profit or go out of business. *"Union Made in America"* is not an economic reality, given globalization and technology. Gone are the days of the workers versus management mentality. Labor must accept that to survive and prosper, they must become productive partners with business, not anti-productive adversaries. Welcome to the new reality!

The only stability is in the public sector. Organized labor contributes extensively to political parties and campaigns, and therefore politicians do not want to bite the hand that feeds them! They placidly support government union organizing or remain neutral. Government services are not profit motivated and taxpayers support the increased labor costs.

An unintended consequence of public sector unions can be an entrenched bureaucracy where it is extremely difficult to terminate underperforming employees. The stereotype of lazy government workers is legendary. When you compound the union job protection clauses, it can become the perfect storm for incompetence. Some union contracts can protect low productivity workers, support poor employee work ethics, and enable incompetency. The system rewards longevity and not productivity. The bureaucracy outlives the bureaucrats.

Foreign automakers (such as Honda and Toyota) are awarded tax incentives to build domestic factories, usually in lower wage states. The foreign automakers create blue-collar and white-collar jobs in states with high unemployment, low union saturation, and can improve the prevailing area wages. This can raise the local standards of living, and increases the tax base, which in turn may help the local economy. It is a winning situation for all parties. The plants tend to be staffed with younger, non-union, less costly workers, and therefore the retirement and health care liabilities for the employers are less expensive. The legacy automakers are usually saddle with archaic union work rules, and staffed with unionized, older, higher paid workers, with expensive health care and retirement benefits.

If unions are to succeed and remain relevant, employers need to view workers and unions, not just as costs factors, but also as productive partners. A modern employer and progressive labor union, working together, and not as adversaries, can achieve higher productivity, and higher wages, with increased competitiveness and higher corporate profitability.

A case in point is the comparison between Costco and Sam's Club (a Wal-Mart company). Both firms sell similar products to similar customers, and are aggressive competitors. Costco's labor costs are about 40% higher than Sam's Club is. In 2005, Costco's operating profit per employee was $21,805, as compared to Sam's Club of $11,615, and Costco's sales per square foot was $866, compared to $525 for Sam's Club. Moreover, Costco's employee turnover rate was only 6%, as compared to 21% for Sam's Club. Profit, productivity, and unionization can be positively related, if all partners work in concert. (Economic Policy Institute Briefing Paper. Unions, the Economy, and the Employee Free Choice Act. Briefing Paper #181. Shaiken, Harley. 2007).

One of the roles of government is to distribute economic prosperity to the workers who are both a major contributor and a major benefactor. Business and labor are mutually dependent on each other, and their success is based on a cooperative positive relationship. A company that fails to be profitable because of out dated and unrealistic labor policies, soon consolidates, files for bankruptcy or closes shop, and the workers loose. An empty factory or closed store does not need workers. Simply put, no employer, no employees!

The American Dream, and thus the nation's *"American Dream"* of economic prosperity are co-dependent on productive labor relations. Globalization, outsourcing, downsizing, technology, and the internet are real threats to the American blue-collar worker. *"Union Made in America"* has become a history lesson, and now might mean, at best, *"Maybe Partially Assembled in America."* A realistic economic alternative is a mutually dependent labor and management relationship, with government acting as a helpful *"consigliore"* or counselor and advisor to both sides.

Government plays a role in American prosperity, by establishing and developing economic initiatives that benefit workers, and support economic growth policies. Government institutes macroeconomic policies to support long-term job creation, and to provide the tools to educate, train and support workers and their families. Microeconomic policies, such as local job creation requires the sustained support of government, industry, and unions, to provide the education, training, and career paths to create jobs consistent with the economy, industry and community needs.

All workers need to earn a living wage, in order to support a family and to grow the economy. Workers at the lower end of the wage scale, require larger social services supports, and contribute little to the economic wellbeing of the nation as a whole. Raising the federal minimum wage to a level that may actually support a family is an example of a government policy that may positively affect families, and in the long term the nation. To keep up with the real purchasing power, wages must be relative to the local economy. Higher wages provide benefits to society, by increasing the families buying power, which stimulates production and consumption, and reduces dependency on social services and government programs.

Lifetime employment, if it ever really existed in the United States, is an outdated concept and does not connect with a fast changing global environment. Advances in technology and economic global competitive realities have reduced the power of the unionized rank-and-file worker, and increase the pressure of management to increase corporate profitability. This has fundamentally changed the nature of work. No longer does an employee expect to spend their entire working lives with one employer, and retire with a gold watch and a small pension for a lifetime of service!

Labor unions understand the needs of the workers, but few unions understand and accept the needs of business. This is a very important concept often ignored. When an employer does not earn a profit, the business will be out of business, and does not need workers. The American and global economies are interconnected and severely distressed. The reality is the old ways of doing business do not work in the new global market place. Labor unions need to become value added partners with business, not an adversary to economic survival.

The labor unions versus management mindset will lead to labor without a place to work, because management has reduced production, merged, or moved the industry to a lower cost environment. *"If unions are going to survive and prosper in the 21st century, we still need to meet the needs of workers, but we also need to find a way to serve important business needs... We can no longer simply demand that business adapt to our needs. We need to adapt to the needs of business..."*

(http://www.virginiaclassifieds.com/biz/virginiabusiness/magazine/yr2006/dec06/ideas.shtml)

The nature of work has changed, and unions must change to meet the depressed global economies and new market demands. The key to long-term survival, industry saturation, increased economic strength, and political power lies in the ability to adapt to changes. In other words, organized labor must become value added partners and productive allies with business, and part of the solution, not part of the problem. To do less will result in a decayed organized labor business model creating its own irrelevance, and in that case, labor unions may soon go the way of the dinosaurs.

"If organized labor continues to do what it has always done,
it will continue to get less than it has always got."
-Anonymous-

Table of Contents

Abstract v

Executive Summary vii

Chapter 1 - Introduction 1
Hypothesis 1
Problem Statement 1

Chapter 2 - Organized Labor Background 5
Business Model Definition: 5
Business Plan and Business Model 5
Labor Union Defined 6
The National Labor Relations Board (NLRB) 7
How Unions Represent Employees 10
Historical Perspective of the Union Business Model 12
Union Business Model Structures 13
Collective Bargaining 14
Historical Perspective of Labor Unions 15

Chapter 3 - Methodology 21
Literature Review 21

Chapter 4 - Data Analysis 25
The Economics of Organized Labor 25
The Economics of Higher Union Wages 27
The Economics of Labor Strikes 29
The Economics of Unions and Wages 30
Unions Raise Non-Union Wages 33
Right-to-Work Laws and Union Wages 34

The Economic Decline of the American Middle Class 37
The Role of Government and Economic Prosperity 39
Job Training 42
Union Job Banks 44
Paid Not To Work 45
Blue-Collar Blues 47
Union Dues and Per Capita Taxes 48
Average Union Dues in 2004 and Union Dues Growth
from 2000 to 2004 51
Union Statistics 53
Largest Labor Unions in the United States: 53
Top 10 blue-collar jobs based on salary medians and
expected growth by 2014: 54
Union Membership and Income Down 55

Chapter 5 – Globalization of Union Jobs 61
Globalization and the Unionized Blue-Collar Worker 61
Globalization Defined 65
Downsizing and Corporate Culture 65
Culture Reinforcing and Culture DestabilizingDownsizing
Practice 67
Outsourcing Union Jobs 68
Transformation of the Labor Market to
Outsourcing Model 70
Offshoring Jobs 72
Privatization of Public Service 76
The Pros and Cons of Privatization 79
Reasons for Using the Private Sector 79
Major Arguments for Opposing Privatization 80
A report by the National Commission for Employment
Policy (1989) found: 81

Chapter 6 - Organize to Survive 83
Organize or Perish 83
Counter Union Organizing Methods 84

The Roles of Labor Relations Consultants or
Union Busters 86
A Workplace Scenario 90
One-on-One Meetings 91
First Contracts and Decertifying a Union 94
Love Tactics and Scare Tactics 96
Expected Time Line of Events 97
Myths and Facts about Unions 101
After the Vote 102
Weingarten Rights 104

Chapter 7 – Politics and Labor Unions 107
Unions and Political Money 107
Union PAC Contributions to Federal Candidates
2003-2004 Election Cycle 108
Election Cycle Spending from 1990 to 2006 109
Top 20 Union Contributors PACs in 2006 110

Important Legal Decisions Affecting the
Labor Business Model 111
The Beck Decision 111
Davenport Decision 113
Kentucky River Decision 114

Organized Labor Political Activities 116
RESPECT Act 116
Employee Free Choice Act (EFCA) 117
Immigration and Labor Unions 122
Immigration by the Numbers 125
NAFTA 127
NAFTA Super Highway 128
Mexican Trucks on U.S. Highways 131

Chapter 8 - Conclusion 133

Bibliography 141

CHAPTER 1

Introduction

Hypothesis

The hypothesis poses the question:
<u>Is Organized Labor A Decaying Business Model</u>?

Problem Statement

To test the hypothesis, the book will examine the organized labor business model from the perspectives of the economic and political influences of organized labor relative to the domestic and global economies.

The traditional organized labor business model, as we have known it over the past century, is not sustainable in it present form, and will become less relevant, irrelevant or extinct, unless major changes are enacted. The author will examine the economic and political issues organized labor faces as it relates to the global economy, for instance outsourcing, downsizing, and technology advancements. One has only to read the newspaper to see examples of labors steady decline in membership, social acceptance, political power, and industry saturation.

IS ORGANIZED LABOR A DECAYING BUSINESS MODEL?

The nature of work has changed, and labor unions have failed to evolve with this change, just as dinosaurs became extinct because they were not able to evolve with the climatic changes. Historically, unions have encouraged an adversarial approach to business operations. It is the 'us' (workers) versus 'them' (management) mentality.

Union representation serves a very important business and economic function. Employees dissatisfied with their employer have few alternatives. They can join a union, accept the working conditions of the employer, or find another job. Companies with poor management skills dealing with their employees are predisposed to create strong labor union employee relationships. *An important business model for companies to follow is treat employees poorly, they will unionize for protection, treat them well, and they will not seek union protection.* Unhappy employees are less productive, produce lower quality products or services, which create a decline in operational efficiencies and in the end are more expensive. When you add a third party labor union to this mix, for the employer, the costs rise, as do unproductive work rules.

On the other hand, happy employees are more productive, produce higher quality goods and services at a lower cost. Satisfied employees take pride in their work, resulting in less employee turnover, fewer work related accidents, and lower absenteeism, because they are rewarded for their work, and feel an ownership in their company and pride in their careers. One must remember historically, union collective bargaining, brought the eight-hour workday, better health care, and built the America middle class.

Organized labor is attempting to stage a come back, with the Change to Win (CtW) split from the old line AFL-CIO, and the Employee Free Choice Act (EFCA) initiative, as examples. Traditional blue-collar unions have experienced a steady decline in dues paying membership, industry saturation, and political power. A semblance of stability is found in niche markets and public sector unions. Even the public sector labor unions are in decline as governments on all levels, are faced with the economic realities of reduced budgets, increased demand for better quality services and an aging workforce.   It can be argued, that the time-honored government employee work ethic and public sector labor unions together help support the culture of mediocrity, encourage inefficiency and bureaucracy, and reward those who are not willing or able to innovate. Essentially longevity is rewarded and productivity is discouraged.

Organized labor is very big business, with *"union income over $10 billion per year"* (http://www.unionfreeamerica.com/dues-forpolitics.htm). If unions were publicly traded companies, the balance sheets of AFL-CIO and the larger unions are impressive, and would command high stock prices. For labor to grow, it must organize and create more dues paying members. Dues paying union membership are the lifeblood of the labor movement. They are the major income source and reason for being. The concept is similar to any business that must constantly seek new accounts to grow and prosper. The mantra is *"<u>Organize or Perish</u>."* This is the basic business model for labor growth. Old industries are collapsing or consolidating and older workers are dying. Organized labor needs new industries and new members, because the larger the base of unionized workers the stronger the economic power and political influence. The alternative is less relevance, irrelevance, or extinction.

Organized labor still wields strong political power, has the ability to bring out large voting blocks for candidates that support its goals, and can bring down opposing candidates. Organized labor is pushing the Employee Free Choice Act (EFCA) through Congress and the Senate. EFCA if enacted as labor wishes will change the landscape of union organizing from secret ballot elections, to an open election through simple card check recognition. Unions will be able to organize more workers, in more industries, easier and eliminate the contentious roadblocks to organizing, and thus grow stronger, faster, and more powerful. Management organizations generally oppose the EFCA, for the reasons unions support it. It is considered in the best interest of corporate America to remain union free, and the EFCA would increase and strengthen unionization.

The future is yet to be written. The past ways of labor and management relationships will not work in a global economy, where outsourcing, downsizing, and technology are the methods of doing business. It is cheaper to make the products in China and ship it to Cincinnati than to manufacturer the product in Cincinnati. "_Union Made in America_" is not an economic reality given the global economy. Employee's interests will always need to be represented, just as employers interests will always need to be represented. If labor unions are to succeed and not become less relevant, irrelevant, or extinct, then unions must change with the global marketplace, and become productive partners with corporate America. The bottom line is that organized labor must accept that the nature of work has changed, and pro-actively work towards that change for the benefit of all parties. To do less, will result in organized labor going the way of the dinosaurs, which were unable to adjust to climatic changes.

CHAPTER 2

Organized Labor Background

Business Model Definition:

A business model is a method used by a company or organization "... spelling out how a company makes money by specifying where it is positioned in the value chain." (http://www.audience-dialogue.org/busmod.html). Another definition states: "A business model is a conceptual tool that contains a set of elements and their relationships and allows expressing the business logic of a specific firm. It is a description of the value a company offers to one or several segments of customers and of the architecture of the firm and its network of partners for creating, marketing, and delivering this value and relationship capital, to generate profitable and sustainable revenue streams." (http://business-model-design.blogspot.com/2005/11/what-is-business-model.html).

Business Plan and Business Model

There is a difference between a _business plan_ and a _business model_. A _business plan_ is a large detailed document, which includes financial objectives and projections. Banks and lending institutions demand business plans as part of the loan requirements, because they want to determine the viability of the enterprise and the ability of the business to repay the loan. A *business model* is a single concept and simple document, usually less than one page, and *"describes the specific way the business expects to make money"* (http://www.audiencedialogue.org/busmod.html).

Innovation is the key to success and a *business model* must allow for innovative opportunities. For example, America On Line (AOL) developed a very successful business model by bringing the World Wide Web to the people, and transformed email from a business tool, to daily use. The mail order business model has been around before the Sears catalogue, but Dell Computer refined the concept of mass customization, and merged an old marketing tool with a new product. The first discount airline business model was Easy Jet. It failed, but the value proposition concept was refined by Jet-Blue, Southwest, and Air-Tran. Google innovated the web search engine, and created specific advertising targeted to the end user. Wal-Mart innovated the retail store concept, and as a result has become the worlds largest discount retailer. Competition forces businesses to become innovative or perish. The same concept holds for labor unions.

A *business model* must be competitive by being innovative, and must allow flexibility to seek new economic opportunities. The buggy whip is a classic example of a business model that failed to innovate, because the industry failed to change with the advent of the horseless carriage, and perished. Organized labor must be innovative, quickly change with the times, and recognize that they must be value added partners with business, not adversaries. The alternative is to go the way of the buggy whip makers, become irrelevant, and perish.

Labor Union Defined

A labor union can best be described as a united group of employees organized together to improve working conditions, economic benefits and respect, through the process of collective bargaining with the employer. Historically, union collective bargaining built the middle class in America. The union middle class is a major economic force that consumes a vast majority of the goods and services they produce.

The growth business model for organized labor is to organize unions in workplaces and industries that are non-union, or have low union saturation. In other words, innovate into new markets. Increased membership strengthens the economic, political, and social power of organized labor. The primary income sources for unions are union dues, and more members equals more money, which give unions more power to influence policies and win elections.(http://www.usw.org/usw/program/content/291.php).

Merriam Webster's Collegiate Dictionary defines labor union as *"an organization of workers formed for the purpose of advancing its members' interests in respect to wages, benefits, and working conditions."* (Merriam Webster's Collegiate Dictionary, Tenth Edition, 1997). The World Book Dictionary further defines a labor union as *"a group of workers joined to protect and promote their interests, especially by dealing as a group with their employer."* A labor organization is defined as *"any group of workers legally empowered to deal with employers on labor disputes, grievances, or conditions of employment, especially as a labor union."* (The World Book Dictionary, 1977).

The National Labor Relations Board (NLRB)

The National Labor Relations Board is *"...an independent federal agency created by Congress in 1935 to administer the National Labor Relations Act, the primary law governing relations between unions and employers in the private sector. The statute guarantees the right of employees to organize and to bargain collectively with their employers, and to engage in other protected concerted activity with or without a union, or to refrain from all such activity."* (http://www.nlrb.gov/).

◄ IS ORGANIZED LABOR A DECAYING BUSINESS MODEL?

The President of the United States appoints the NLRB Board members for a five-year term. The General Counsel, appointed by the President, confirmed by the Senate, for a four-year term, is responsible for investigating and prosecuting unfair labor practice cases. (http://www.cftech.com/BrainBank/HUMANRESOURCES/NatlLabRelBd.html).

The NLRB has two main functions. It permits employees to decide, by a secret ballot election, if they wish to have union representation at their workplace, and if so, which union they choose. The other function is to prevent or remedy unfair labor practices by either employers or unions, and place restrictions on employers and unions in conducting business with employees and each other. In its purest form, it provides employee protection from harassments and discrimination because of their lawful union activity. An aggrieved party must file a case with the NLRB, as regulated by law.

The National Labor Relations Board (NLRB) administers the National Labor Relations Act (NLRA), which is intended to benefit labor. Labor unions maintain that employers benefit more than employees do, because employers have learned to manipulate the law to their advantage. Employees have rights under Section 7 of the National Labor Relations Act, such as:

- Forming or attempting to form a union among the employees of a company.
- Joining a union whether the employer recognizes the union or not.
- Assisting a union to organize the employees of an employer.
- Going out on strike to secure better working conditions.
- Refraining from activity on behalf of a union.

(http://www.nlrb.gov/Workplace_Rights/i_am_new_to_this_website/what_is_the_national_labor_relations_act.aspx).

The National Labor Relations Act (NLRA) forbids employers: "...from interfering with, restraining, or coercing employees in

ORGANIZED LABOR BACKGROUND

the exercise of rights relating to organizing, forming, joining or assisting a labor organization for collective bargaining purposes, or engaging in concerted activities, or refraining from any such activity. Similarly, labor organizations may not re-strain or coerce employees in the exercise of these rights." (http://www.nlrb.gov/nlrb/shared_files/brochures/engulp.pdf).

Employers cannot legally threaten employees with loss of jobs or benefits if they join a union or engage in a protected activity. Employers cannot threaten to close a plant if the company becomes unionized. However, employers can *predict* a plant closing, cutbacks or downsizing, as long as it is not a *threat*. Employers cannot legally question employees about union sympathies, coerce, or restrain employees engaging in protected activities. Further, employers cannot legally promise benefits, promotions, or salary increases if they vote against the union, or threaten to transfer, lay-off, terminate or reassign employees because of their union activities. Labor unions argue that reality is different from the law, as employers have learned to use the law to their advantage, with little retribution.

On the other side of the coin, unions cannot threaten employees with job loss, job reduction, or pay, if they do not join the union, or refuse to process a grievance because the employee is critical of the union. The union cannot have an employee discharged for not complying with the labor agreements, as long as the employee is paying dues. The union cannot legally give preference for job hiring or referral based on race, or union activity. (http://www.nlrb.gov/nlrb/shared_files/brochures/engrep.asp).

The National Labor Relations Act specifically excludes certain classes of employees:
- Employed as agricultural laborers.
- Employed in the domestic service of any person or family in a home.
- Employed by a parent or spouse.
- Employed as an independent contractor.

- Employed as a supervisor.
- Employed by an employer subject to the Railway Labor Act.
- Employed by a Federal, State, or local government.
- Employed by any other person who is not an employer as defined in the NLRA.

In addition, the NLRA does not enforce various federal laws within the jurisdiction of the Department of Labor, for example:

- Fair Labor Standards Act.
- *Wage Garnishment Provisions of Various Statutes.*
- *Public Contracts Act.*
- *Service Contract Act.*
- *Davis-Bacon and Related Acts.*
- *Contract Work Hours and Safety Standards Act.*

The NLRA does not interfere with various state laws relating to employment:

- Unemployment Compensation Statutes.
- Workman's Compensation Statutes.
- Equal Employment Statutes.
- Various statutes within the Equal Employment Opportunity Commission.

(http://www.nlrb.gov/nlrb/shared_files/brochures/engulp.pdf).

How Unions Represent Employees

A <u>card check</u> are authorization cards, or petitions, distributed by the union, and proving to the government, that the union has a majority support of the eligible workers (known as *50% plus 1* rule, that is 50% of the eligible employees plus 1), which creates a simple majority of the employees within the company or a business unit. The procedure, known as a <u>card check election</u>, can allow the union to become the employee bargaining agent, without an election, if the employer voluntarily accepts union representation. *(The National Labor Relations Board and You-Unfair Labor Practices* pamphlet available on line at http://www.nlrb.gov/nlrb/shared_files/brochures/engrep.asp). The Employee Free Choice Act will utilize the *card check* system as the primary unionization method.

An <u>authorization card</u> is a signed and dated union card filled out by pro-union workers, during a union representation campaign, specifying that union as the collective bargaining agent of the employees. The National Labor Relations Board requires a minimum of 30% of the employees' signatures on the cards, as a showing of interest, before it will conduct an election. Unions usually will not file for an election unless a strong majority of the potential bargaining unit members has signed authorization cards. Union organizing campaigns are not easy to win and require large financial and staff investments. Labor unions need to have employee solidarity to win elections, strength in numbers, and enthusiastic pro-union activists willing to fight to win.

In cases where an employer is determined to remain <u>union free</u>, the pro-union organizing campaigns, and the company anti-union organizing campaigns start, with the outcome usually determined by the NLRB election, and possibly various court actions. The psychological war begins before the union drive begins, and a union organizing drive can be an emotional experience in which co-workers, supervisors, managers, and friends become polarized. Working relationships and personal relationships become strained and morale can suffer as a result. The process is very expensive, divisive, and labor intensive for the company and the union.

The union is determined to win and become the legally recognized bargaining agent for the employees. Unions must win elections to gain membership, thereby giving organized labor saturation, political power, and economic strength. Union dues collected from represented employees are a major source of income.

IS ORGANIZED LABOR A DECAYING BUSINESS MODEL?

For the company, the cost can be measured financially, emotionally, and in the loss of worker productivity. Company supervisors and management energies and resources are directed towards the union campaign, and away from the business of running the business. Business suffers, clients, customers and suppliers may refrain from doing business until the situation is resolved, income is lower, expenses are higher, and other union and non-union competitors usually benefit. For these reasons, companies may choose to accept <u>card check elections</u>, hoping that positive employer and employee relationships may outweigh the costs of waging an all out anti-union campaign. This is an individual business decision based on the needs of the stakeholders.

<u>Historical Perspective of the Union Business Model</u>

In 1776, the Declaration of Independence was signed in the Carpenters Hall of the Philadelphia Guild of Carpenters. The oldest form of the <u>union business model</u> was the associations of skilled workers, which evolved in the United States in the 1700's and 1800's. They formed <u>guilds of artisans</u>, known as <u>Guilds</u>, such as the masons, carpenters, cabinetmakers, shoemakers, leatherworkers, printers, and similar skilled trades. (http://www.usw.org/usw/program/content/291.php). The first <u>labor strike</u> was the printers in 1794, for shorter hours and better pay, followed by the cabinetmakers in 1796, carpenters in 1797, and cordwainers (leatherworkers) in 1799. (http://www.socialstudieshelp.com/Eco_Unionization.htm).

The United States economy was primarily based on agricultural, with the majority of the population living on farms and small towns, until the later part of the 1800's. The industrial revolution of the late 19th and 20th century changed the nation from rural to urban. As factories and manufacturing grew, the farmers moved to the cities and became factory workers. These were primarily unskilled or low skilled and low paying jobs, such as machine operators and clothing workers. Men, women, and children were working in sweatshops, ill fed, and living in tenement housing in crowded cities.

The *labor union business model* gained strength after the Civil War and became stronger during the Industrial Revolution. Workers formed unions in response to health and safety concerns, such as very long hours (14 hour days, 6 days per week were considered normal), dangerous working conditions, child labor, and very low wages. Historically, labor unions thrive when workers are mistreated, and oppressed. Labor unions united these workers, and over time, helped force changes, by improving working conditions, and child labor laws, raising wages, reducing work hours, enhancing workers health, and safety (http://usinfo.state.gov/products/pubs/oecon/chap9.htm).

The United States is a nation born from a struggle to be free from oppression. Labor unions were born from the working persons desires for respect, dignity, and to earn a fair wage for their labors. The slogan *"a fair wage for a fair days work,"* was a rallying cry. Historically, labor unions have provided economic and legal protection from abusive employers, raised the standards of living, and helped create the American middle class.

Union Business Model Structures

Union business models follow various structures. *Craft unions* represent a specific craft or trade, such as carpenters or leatherworkers. *Industrial unions* organize workers from a specific industry, such automotive, steel, or railroads, while *general unions* have workers from a cross section of skills. These unions organized as *locals*, representing a state, location, or region of the country. The locals form *national* or *federation* unions, which combine to become *international* unions. *Social unionisms*, mostly found in Europe, are usually allied with a political party. They are organized to create political reforms, and legislative, or social activism. A *service model* union focuses on member services, dispute resolution, and workers rights, while an *organizing model* concentrates on organizing new workers and industries. Unions often combine business models to serve their members needs. (http://www.reference.com/search?q=labor%20unions).

There are various union operating models or union shop types in the workplace. In a *closed shop,* the employer can only hire union members in good standing. A *hiring hall* is a union location or hall, where an employer must hire workers through the union directly. A *union shop* can hire non-union workers, but they must join the union within a specific period. In an *agency shop* or the *Rand Formula*, workers must pay an agency fee to the union for the services the union provides, such as contract negotiations. *Fair share* laws, usually involving state government employees, make it easier for unions to collect agency fees. An *open shop* union employment environment does not require employees to be union members or contribute to the union or the collective bargaining process. (http://www.reference.com/search?q=labor%20unions). *Right-to-work laws* are laws in 22 states, known as *right-to-work-states*, under provisions of the Taft-Hartley Act, which prohibit union membership or paying union dues or fees as a condition of employment. (http://www.reference.com/browse/wiki/Right-to-work_law).

Collective Bargaining

Collective bargaining is defined as "...*union negotiations on behalf of a group of workers in relation to pay and conditions of employment. If negotiations breakdown, the dispute may result in industrial action (strike) or may be referred to arbitration...*" (http://www.reference.com/search?q=collective%20bargaining)

Collective bargaining, or *group bargaining*, was first established in Great Britain in the nineteenth century. The National Labor Relations Act in 1935, (Wagner Act) established the right to collective bargaining. It is a method for the employer, and unions representing the collective employees, to negotiate and resolve issues, such as wages, working conditions, job safety, employer and employee rights, the right to organize workers and recognize the union. The negative aspect of collective bargaining is it can deprive workers of the right to negotiate individually for their services. If a worker has special skills or abilities, they are not able to command a higher wage than their peers are. The positive position is that without union protection and collective bargaining, the employee loses power and control to protect their rights, and is at the mercy of the employer. Collective bargaining sets the basis for labor contracts and agreements between management and workers.

<u>Labor contracts</u> are very specific legal working agreements between management and labor that describe in detail the standards, rights, privileges and expectations of all parties. When one side or the other breaks a contract condition, the aggrieved side has legal methods and specific rights to try to settle their difference. This may involve fines, arbitration, sanctions, or strikes, or other methods as called for in the labor contract, prescribed by acceptable labor law and practices, or adjudicated by court. Collective bargaining and union labor contracts are enforceable by law, and are very powerful legal and economic tools. (http://www.reference.com/search?q=Labor%20contract).

<u>Historical Perspective of Labor Unions</u>

The Knights of Labor formed in 1869 was a federation, or organization of local unions. Unions understood to succeed, the concept of *"United We Stand, Separate We Fall"* required unions to unite to become a stronger and more powerful advocate for workers rights. The Knights of Labor accepted all members, skilled and unskilled labor, black and white, male, and female. This was a radical concept following the mood of the country after the Civil

IS ORGANIZED LABOR A DECAYING BUSINESS MODEL?

War and the end of slavery. Membership reached 750,000, but conflicts between the skilled and unskilled workers and the loss of unity contributed to their downfall. The Knights of Labor set the stage for other federation of labor unions.

The next union to emerge was the Federation of Organized Trades and Labor Unions in 1881. Samuel Gompers of the Cigar Makers Union, who later formed the American Federation of Labor (AFL), fought for the eight-hour workday. In 1886, the Federation stated, *"… the eight hours shall constitute a legal day's labor…"* (http://www.albany.edu/history/history316/LaborMovementHistory1.html).

The United Mine Workers in 1898, won the eight-hour workday, followed in 1900, by the Building Trades Council, whose motto was *"eight hours for $3 per day."* The printing trades established the eight-hour workday in 1905. In 1914, Ford Motor Company, reduced the workday to eight hours and doubled the pay to $5 per day, and as a result, productivity increased. The first federal law establishing the eight-hour workday for railroad workers, with additional pay for overtime, was the Adamson Act in 1917. Under the New Deal in 1938, the Fair Labor Standards Act set minimum wages, and made working eight hours per day the legal national requirement for all employees. (http://www.reference.com/browse/wiki/Eight-hour_day).

In 1886, Samuel Gompers formed the American Federation of Labor (AFL), as a union of only skilled workers. The AFL expressed their beliefs in this statement: *"The various trades have been affected by the introduction of machinery, the subdivision of labor, the use of women's and children's labor and the lack of an apprentice system-so that the skilled trades were rapidly sinking to the level of pauper labor. To protect the skilled labor of America from being reduced to beggary and to sustain the standard of American workmanship and skill, the trades unions of America have been established."* (http://www.socialstudieshelp.com/Eco_Unionization.htm).

ORGANIZED LABOR BACKGROUND

The American Federation of Labor business model is a decentralized craft union of skilled single occupation workers, with members belonging to an affiliated local or national union. The AFL advocated *"business or pure and simple unionism"* (http://www.reference.com/search?q=labor%20unions), that is improving working conditions through collective bargaining, fighting for higher wages, shorter hours, laws against child labor, and for workmen's compensation and the eight hour workday. The AFL, had grown to over 10 million members, and became the largest labor federation when it merged with the Congress of Industrial Organization (CIO) in 1955. (http://www.reference.com/search?q=American%20Federation%20of%20Labor).

In 1935, John L Lewis formed the Congress of Industrial Organization (CIO), which grew from a dispute with the AFL over organizing industrial workers. The AFL was a craft union, while the CIO wanted to unionize all the workers in an industry, (such as the steel or automotive industries), regardless of skills or crafts. The craft workers disliked industrial workers, who were less skilled, foreign born, minorities, or African American. The CIO embraced these workers, was more aggressive and militant than the AFL. As a result, the CIO grew rapidly from 1936 to 1945. The methodology was to unionize all the workers in a plant under one union, rather than weaken labor's power by dividing the workers into separate crafts. The philosophy of *"United We Stand, Divided We Fall"* prevailed, and showed employers the CIO had strength in numbers. (http://www.reference.com/search?r=13&q=Congress%20of%20Industrial%20Organizations).

In 1955, the CIO merged with the AFL and became the AFL-CIO. In 2005, the federation represented more than 10 million workers. Once again, the motto *"United We Stand, Divided We Fall"* was a viable business model and more than a slogan. For the next 50 years (1955 to 2005), the AFL-CIO has represented a majority of union workers in the United States. Membership is not restricted to craft or industry and is often referred to as the *House* of Labor. (http://www.reference.com/search?q=AFL-CIO%20).

In 2005, the Change to Win Federation was formed from seven unions that broke from the AFL-CIO, and represented about 35% of the membership base of the AFL-CIO. At the beginning of the twenty-first century, labor union membership and union density, a measurement of the percentage of unionized workers, had reduced to less than 8% of private sector workers, and only 12% of all unionized workers, down from 30% of all workers in the 1950's. The Change to Win (CtW) coalition was dissatisfied with the AFL-CIO business model, and felt the organizing business model was the key to union growth. In other words, for labor unions to grow and not become irrelevant or perish, unions had to organize new workers and industries that previously had been non-union.

The Change to Win (CtW) coalition was based on the following principals: *"Working people, including current union members, cannot win consistently without uniting millions more workers in unions, and every worker in America has the right to a union that has the focus, strategy, and resources to unite workers in that industry and win."* (http://www.reference.com/search?q=change%20to%20win)

The Change to Win (CtW) business model is an organizing business model. For example, organize all the workers in a specific industry, such as hotel, office cleaning, and food service workers, not just specific job categories with in an industry. Change to Win believes in spending resources organizing the unorganized, and merging smaller unions together to form larger and more powerful unions, with the ultimate goals of achieving union strength, power and industry saturation. Historically, union strength has been in manufacturing and heavy industry. The non-union industries are primarily service sector, such as hotels, office cleaning, and food services. These industries tend to pay lower wages and have a large immigrant, minority, and female employment base. (http://www.reference.com/search?q=change%20to%20win).

Union membership in the US breaks down to the following numbers:
- AFL: 9,000,000+
- Change to Win (CtW): 6,000,000+

(www.reference.com).

American labor unions have changed American politics. Politicians embrace labor unions, because labor unions can get out the vote for the politician or party that supports the needs of the labor unions. Organized labor still is a powerful voting block, a strong ally, and a formidable enemy. However, union political strength has declined as its membership base, income, and industry saturation has declined.

Historically the labor movement has been male dominated. There is a slogan of some merit, which attributes the decline in the labor movement, to the fact that organized labor has become *"Male, Pale, and Stale."* Essentially the labor movement has been white male dominated, and that is one of many reasons for the decline of organized labor in the United States. The Change to Win coalition, has embraced low wage immigrant, and minority segments of the working population that previously has not been welcomed in traditional unions. The face of labor is changing, as is the nature of work.

As the nature of work has changed, the nature of the workers has changed. Today's workforce is no longer, *"Male, Pale, and Stale."* Today's workforce are more likely to be younger, female, foreign born, multi-lingual, and people of color. Union density has rapidly declined, as the economy has moved from industrial, to service based, and towards informational and technology based. Outsourcing, downsizing, privatization, technology, and the global economy are some of the threats to the traditional organized labor business model. It is vital for organized labor to overcome these threats if it is to prosper in the centuries to follow. The alternative is the demise of organized labor.

CHAPTER 3

Methodology

Literature Review

The literature review and research documentation for this paper comes from numerous internet and print sources. The author writes from the perspective of participant observer, active in organizing actions involving two national broadcast facilities, as union shop steward for a public housing authority, representing union employees in contract disputes, on the Labor-Management Relations Committee (LMRC), and on the labor contract negotiating committee.

The hallmark of labor relations is working with various groups of people, each with different agendas, and arriving at a fair consensus. The *labor* versus *management (us* versus *them)* business model may have worked well in the early twentieth century, but will not work in the twenty first century and beyond. Modern unionism requires a customer and employer centric approach, and labor must act as partners with industries, not as adversaries.

The author maintains a moderate union perspective, understands, and respects the positions of both labor and management. Success in a technologically advanced and modern global society

IS ORGANIZED LABOR A DECAYING BUSINESS MODEL?

lies in a bilateral and bipartisan approach to solving labor and management problems and finding mutually acceptable solutions. The author's intentions are to present an objective analysis of the issues and challenges facing organized labor.

The book poses the question "*Is Organized Labor a Decaying Business Model?*" and will examine the economic and political issues organized labor faces relative to the global economy, such as outsourcing, downsizing, and technology advancements. Labor unions face huge challenges if they are to succeed for future generations. Failure will result in less relevance, irrelevance, or extinction. The key for organized labors survival and long-term growth lies in organizing, and adapting to changes. Unions must become productive allies with business, and be part of the solutions, not part of the problems.

The author will examine the methods organized labor uses to earn money and how it allocates funds for administrative, political, and organizing costs. Taken as a single entity, if labor unions were publicly traded companies, they would command high stock values. Organized labor is very big business, with *"union income over $10 billion per year"* (http://www.unionfreeamerica.com/duesforpolitics.htm).

Downsizing, outsourcing, offshoring, privatization, globalization, and technology are major issues facing organized labor. As the economy has moved from agrarian, to industrial, to service, and is transforming towards technological and internet information based, labor unions have failed to keep up. The cost of doing business in the United States exceeds the marketplace. It is more cost effective to have customer call centers in India than in Indiana. Globalization has placed extensive downward pressure on raw materials, labor costs, manufacturing costs, and, the prices for goods and services.

Wal-Mart is a prime example of a retail company utilizing globalization. The company buys products from China and other low costs countries, squeezes price concessions from U.S. suppliers, and pays its employees at the lower end of the wage scale. Other retailers can pay employees less because Wal-Mart pays less. The prices for Wal-Mart products, from food to electronics, are lower which in turn forces smaller retailers out of business. They cannot compete with Wal-Mart's prices, economy of scale, and just-in-time delivery systems. Wal-Mart is so large, they can afford to loose money on selected items to increase store traffic, and therefore increase market share.

Downsizing due to technology and automation in manufacturing jobs has created market forces that effect labor unions ability to controls wages, work rules, and working conditions. The automotive industry is a prime example of downsizing and automation. Robotic machines can perform welding and painting jobs that previously required many well-paid skilled union workers. Automation, the internet and technology, has enabled companies to do more work with fewer workers, and at lower unit cost.

Private sector and government sector employers have found that business functions can be outsourced at lower costs, and more efficiently, than having the work performed in house by company or government employees. The work is outsourced domestically or globally, using independent contractors, who are usually paid on a per unit basis. These workers are cheaper, because they do not receive benefits, and their employment terms are flexible and directly related to the needs of the company. Work is outsourced globally, for example to China, India, Mexico, African and Asian nations, or Caribbean countries. Technology and the internet have had significant impacts on global outsourced work. How many times have you called a customer service center, to be greeted with a message saying "... *for English press one, for Spanish press two, for other languages press three...*" This call is routed via the internet backbone known as VoIP, or Voice over Internet Protocol, to the appropriate language speaking country call center. Welcome to customer service in the global economy!

IS ORGANIZED LABOR A DECAYING BUSINESS MODEL?

The future growth for any business enterprise is to acquire and sustain new customers. The growth business model for labor unions is *organizing*. Unions expand by organizing the unorganized, which is to unionize currently non-union workers in non-union industries. To accomplish this, labor unions must reach out to untapped markets, including workers and industries previously overlooked or underserved by unions.

Companies, when faced with a union organizing drive, have essentially two options. They can accept the unions through the *card check* process, and attempt to negotiate favorable pro-company language in their contract. However, if they wish to remain union free, companies hire labor relations consultants to help convince employees to vote against the labor union. The union organizing and anti-union organizing business model is expensive, resources intensive, and a disruptive for the union, and the company.

Organized labor still wields significant political power, and has the ability to bring out large voting blocks for local, state, and national candidates that support its goals, and bring down opposing candidates. Union workers generally vote, and support Democratic agendas. Labor unions can marshal the support of its vast membership base, such as organize *get-out-the-vote* community drives, and place extensive financial and human capital resources towards goals that affect union centric issues.

Organized labor is pushing the Employee Free Choice Act (EFCA) through the House and the Senate. EFCA, if enacted as labor wishes, will change the landscape of union organizing from the National Labor Relations Board (NLRB) secret ballot elections, to an open union organizing policy, through simple card check recognition. Unions will be able to organize more workers, in more industries, easier and eliminate some of the roadblocks to organizing, and thus grow stronger, faster, and more powerful.

CHAPTER 4

Data Analysis

The Economics of Organized Labor

In a free market economy, employers must pay labor wages in accordance with the prevailing norm for similar workers, with similar skills, in similar industries, or job classifications. <u>Wages are simply the prices paid for human labor, and are determined by the economic laws of supply and demand</u>. Businesses must also pay for raw materials, utilities, physical plant, and other services as the market dictates and in accordance with the comparable norms. If an employer chooses to pay *lower* wages than the competition, for similar work skills and job classifications, the employer will soon find worker shortages or must accept less skilled workers. Generally, less skilled, less educated, or poorly trained workers, tend to produce inferior goods or services at higher costs, with the negative results being lower productivity, higher return rates, and greater customer dissatisfaction. Competitors take advantage of this gap, and eventually the business is out of business.

Workers will seek the best return on their labor investment within their industry, skills set or education. Employers, who choose to pay workers significantly *above* the prevailing wages, will be at an economic disadvantage, as this will increase the expenses for their products, or services, compared to the industry norm. Given this scenario an employer will soon be out of business, or must make up for the extra labor costs by raising prices, or expense reductions in other arenas of their production or service cycle. Consumers, naturally seek the best products or services at the lowest cost, relative to the competition, and consistent with the quality of the goods or services purchased.

The higher American standards of living, are not exclusively caused by labor unions or the political or humanitarian will of the nation, but are based on the economic laws of supply and demand. An employer's need for economic survival and prosperity, require in part, obtaining the best raw materials to produce the goods or services at the lowest cost, consistent with quality, quantity, competitive pressures, and consumer needs. Labor is one of the costs of doing business. Capitalism creates labor demands, and this determines the price employers must pay. Labor unions represent groups of workers collectively, and to this extent can influence wages, benefits, and working conditions. Labor unions do not determine wages. Economic conditions determine wages.

Henry Ford understood the need to attract higher skilled, loyal, and more efficient workers. He paid his manufacturing employees five dollars per day, when the prevailing rates were between two and three dollars per day. He also reduced the workday from nine hours to eight hours, when nine to ten hours were the prevailing norm. He did not do this for great humanitarian reasons or because of labor unions. Henry Ford instituted these standards because he knew that it would increase worker productivity. Higher paid Ford workers could afford to buy his Ford cars and this increased market share for Ford cars. The shorter workday, reduced employee fatigue, reduced production line mistakes, and was more cost effective. It was a business decision determined by economic needs, not humanity, or unions. The eight-hour workday meant he could run two or three equal shifts, and keep his factories working constantly and efficiently. The motive was profit. (http://www.nathanielbranden.com/catalog/articles_essays/labor_unions.html).

The American standard of living is higher than other countries, because the U.S. economic system invests heavily in plant, production, and innovation. Wages are a factor of capital investment. American worker productivity and thus American wages are higher, because U.S. capital investment is higher which requires higher skills, better training, a more educated workforce, and less reliance on unskilled manual labor.

"American wages are higher than wages in other countries because the capital invested per head of the worker is greater and the plants are thereby in the position to use the most efficient tools and machines. American way of life is the result of the fact that the United States has put fewer obstacles in the way of saving and capital accumulation than other nations. The economic backwardness of such countries as India consists precisely in the fact that their policies hinder both the accumulation of capital and the investment of foreign capital. As the capital required is lacking, the Indian enterprises are prevented from employing sufficient quantities of modern equipment, are therefore producing much less per man hour and can only afford to pay wage rates which, compared with American wage rates, appear as shockingly low." (Planning for Freedom, 2nd ed., Libertarian Press, 1962, pp. 151-152). (http://www.nathanielbranden.com/catalog/articles_essays/labor_unions.html)

The Economics of Higher Union Wages

Unions alone do not create higher living standards. Unions can create higher wages above normal free market conditions in targeted industries. This often leads to an imbalance between wages, because unionized workers receive higher wages and non-unionized workers are unable to find decent jobs. In theory, in a

⊰ IS ORGANIZED LABOR A DECAYING BUSINESS MODEL?

free market economy, wages flow to a level in which all qualified workers, seeking work, find work, because the cost of labor is relative to the other costs producing the goods and services. Simply put, when the company profits, the workers have work, and when the company does not profit, the workers are out of work, because the company closes, or reduces production.

The labor-demand-curve (LDC) economic model, suggests that unions seek the highest wages possible, usually outside of the normal wages for similar work in non-unionized industries. Higher wages puts extensive pressure on industry to reduce other costs or raise prices to offset the higher expenses. Industry may choose to reduce total labor costs by reducing the company workforce, introducing automation or technology to replace labor, or by outsourcing certain functions. Higher wages can equate to fewer available jobs. Raising prices to offset higher union labor costs is tricky, because certain products may be sold at higher costs, while other products or services are cost conscious. Price wars put more strain on unionized legacy companies or industries, because their labor cost are less flexible. Raising prices can attract non-union competitors to produce similar goods or services at lower costs, and thus drive the unionized employer out of business. (Princeton University Industrial Relations. *Notes on the Economics of Labor Unions*. Working Paper No. 452. Farber, Henry. Princeton University. May 2001).

The auto industry is an example of a unionized workforce that is <u>not</u> competitive with foreign car companies. The U.S. auto industry has reduced production to try to stay competitive with foreign car manufacturers, and shifts have been cut. The net result is that unionized workers are not working. The auto industry has bought out or terminated many thousands of unionized employees. The United Auto Workers (UAW) union has fewer dues paying members, and therefore is in a weaker bargaining position. The production cutbacks have a ripple effect on parts suppliers and on non-union white-collar administrative and management workers. The labor unions' reason for being has been drastically cut, because historically, wages and associated costs such as benefits, health care, and retirement packages have far exceeded the economic functions of this industry.

The bottom line is that an employer must make a profit, and if wages and benefits disproportionately change the equation, employees, and labor unions both loose. When a business cannot sustain a reasonable profit, it is not able to reinvest in the business. The business or industry are faced with a dilemma: cut back to meet demand, reduce costs by outsourcing or moving production overseas, sell the business, file for bankruptcy and hope to survive and emerge leaner and stronger, or close the business. *"Unemployment is the inevitable result of forcing wage rates above their free market level."* (http://www.nathanielbranden.com/catalog/articles_essays/labor_unions.html).

The workers loose when production cutbacks require employers to reduce shifts or reduce wages. Less work or lower wages, creates a greater burden on health care and public social services, reduces the tax base, and the net result is the overall economy suffers. Less skilled and less educated workers tend to be stronger pro-union advocates, while more educated and higher skilled workers are less likely to unionize.

The Economics of Labor Strikes

When labor and management recognize that a dispute or problem exists, and it may be in the best interests of all parties to resolve the issues as amicably as possibly. Disputes can be resolved by mutual agreement, arbitration, or strikes. Dispute resolution by mutual agreement or arbitration requires a business decision that it is better to solve the problems peacefully and mutually coexist. Arbitration obligates both sides to accept a binding decision from the arbitrator, and without recourse.

The other alternative is a labor strike. Strikes are the avenue of last resort, and in the final analysis, usually both sides may have been better off avoiding a strike. The longer the strike, the more costly it is for labor and management. The business suffers from reduced profits, lost sales, and increased risk that competitors might take advantage of the situation. The strike business model suggests that higher profit firms would prefer to settle the strike quickly. They may be more willing to accept the union demands for higher wages and benefits, in return for a quick settlement, because their daily profit losses are very high. Lower profit firms may be more willing to trade the loss of profits now, for the promise of lower wages, and higher profits, when the strike ends. The union may be willing to accept concessions now, to get back to work, because of the financial and emotional loses suffered by the striking employees and the sponsoring labor union. (Princeton University Industrial Relations. *Notes on the Economics of Labor Unions.* Working Paper No. 452. Farber, Henry. Princeton University. May 2001).

To keep the business viable and to weaken the union resolve, employers need to hire employees for the duration of the strike. Labor unions are very opposed to *strike breakers,* that is, temporary employees hired to replace striking employees. In a pro-labor economy, unemployed workers are not free to hire out for less than the prevailing wage and employers are not free to hire them. *"In the case of strikes, if unemployed workers attempted to obtain the jobs vacated by union strikers, by offering to work for a lower wage, they often would be subjected to threats and physical violence at the hands of union members."* (http://www.nathaniel-branden.com/catalog/articles_essays/labor_unions.html).

The Economics of Unions and Wages

Unions influence wages directly through the collective bargaining process. Unions can also indirectly influence wages. The presence of a union in a local economy or industry can bring up the wages, because other employers need to compete for the same pool of skilled labor. The union and non-union wage differential is known as the _wage gap_. However, the labor business model suggests that non-union workers are lower paid, and derive fewer benefits than union labor. In theory, higher paid union workers, create fewer job opportunities, for other union labor. This _spill over_ creates more workers willing to accept lower non-union wages. Therefore, the economic laws of labor supply and demand, causes lower wages because more people are looking for work. Another wage and labor theory suggests that wages are raised because of the _threat effect_ of unions, as non-union employers raise wages to avoid becoming unionized.

The *wage gap* between unionized and non-union workers has a direct economic effect on labor costs, and therefore the costs of producing a particular goods or service. Labor unions prefer to have wages related to specific job classifications and to apply a standard pay rate for each job classification. Union contracts are built around strong _work rules,_ which control the number of employees and scope of workers needed for a specific job function. Non-union workers have more pay flexibility, as they are rewarded relative to the individual workers skills, personality, and work ethic. Non-union *work rules* are frequently established by the employer, or industry standards, and are based on the number and scope of workers needed to perform a certain job function.

Thus, in a non-union company, for example, a group of machine operators with similar skill sets, could each be earning different wages, and performing different job functions, based on managements perceived employment skills matrix for each individual worker. In a unionized work environment, the same group of machine operators would earn the same wages, and work under the same work rules, unless contract terms called for differentials based on shift, longevity, or other negotiated basis. The result is that in a unionized employer, individual skill is less of a wage factor, while longevity and other negotiated terms, are factors that increase *all* workers wages, not individual workers, in specific job classifications with the employer.

Another factor associated with the *wage gap* between union and non-union firms is the relationships between race, gender, type of industry, and company size. For example, on average, non-whites in non-union jobs earn 8.2% less than non-whites in union jobs do. Non-whites in union jobs earn about 6.1% less than whites do. The union wage gap is larger for non-whites than for whites. Married males in the non-union job market, earn 23.5% more than non-union single males. While, married males in a unionized employment situation earn 9.9% more than single unionized males. Female workers are paid less in both the union and non-union employment. This can partially be attributed to occupational gender segregation, in which female workers are less prevalent in traditional industries or occupations, such as heavy manufacturing as an example.

The *wage gap* is larger for unskilled workers in non-union employers, and the difference is dependent on the skill level required for the jobs, and varies by occupations, geographic locations, and size of the employer. Traditional unionized employers have standardized wage rates tied to the specific job classification, and therefore the *wage gap* is less for skilled and unskilled workers. Generally, larger firms pay higher wages than smaller firms do, and unionized workers in a small firm enjoy a larger pay advantage than unionized workers in a larger firm. Unionized workers, typically earn higher wages, and enjoy better benefits, and employment longevity, than non-unionized workers do.

There are other factors to consider in the *wage gap* scenario that are not directly tied to wages. These factors may include benefits, employment longevity, and layoffs. As an example, unionized workers, on average, enjoy larger benefits packages, such as health insurance, vacations, and pensions. The employment turn over is usually lower in a unionized environment, because wages are higher, better benefits, and employees have a voice, through the union, in workplace issues. A negative factor is that employees are more likely to be laid off in unionized companies, than in non-union firms, because of the higher labor costs, and less employer labor flexibility to adjust to market changes. (Princeton University Industrial Relations. *Notes on the Economics of Labor Unions*. Working Paper No. 452. Farber, Henry. Princeton University. May 2001).

Unions Raise Non-Union Wages

There are two reasons that unions create an effect on non-union employers in terms of wages, benefits, and over all working conditions. The *spill over* creates more workers willing to accept lower non-union wages, resulting in a decrease in union employment due to higher union wages. Increased union wages causes employers to higher fewer workers, which increases the number of available workers in the community. This causes more workers to seek other non-union employment, which in turn, reduces non-union wages in the community. The economic laws of labor supply and demand observe that wages are lower when more people are looking for work. The *spill over* generally applies to less skilled workers, as they have limited marketability.

Most non-union employers wish to remain non-union. Therefore, these employers raise wages, because of the *threat effect* of unionization, as a method to stay union free. In theory, if non-union employers provide improved wages, working conditions, and higher benefits, similar to the union model, the employees will be happy and choose to remain non-union. The automotive industry is an excellent example. The legacy U.S. auto industry is significantly unionized, while the foreign companies with large plants in the U.S., such as Toyota and Honda, are non-union. These companies have remained non-union, because the employers provide comparable wages and working conditions similar to the unionized companies and therefore the employees have not felt the need to become unionized. Non-unionized wages are related to the prevailing wages in the unionized workforce and are directly related to union density in the industry. When an industry is more unionized (union density), similar non-union workers enjoy higher wages, benefits, and improved working conditions, as a residual benefit.

Repressive employers tend to create strong unions. Unhappy workers seek unions for protection, and to improve wages, benefits, and working conditions. Progressive employers create happy employees, and tend to remain non-union. They can remain non-union, as long as the employer continues to treat the workers with respect, and wages, benefits, and working conditions are comparable to the unionized standards in the industry or geographic location. The employer benefits because with a non-union work force, the employer has greater staffing flexibility, and less cumbersome work rules. The non-union employer can operate the business with more flexibility to change shifts, job assignment and production schedules, and can make quick adjustments depending on immediate business needs. In a unionized work environment, the employer has less business flexibility, because a third party (the union) is determining the work rules and production schedules, based on the collective bargaining agreement signed years before. (Princeton University Industrial Relations. Non-Union Wages Rates and the Threat of Unionization. Working Paper No. 472. Farber, Henry. Princeton University. 2003).

Right-to-Work Laws and Union Wages

Twenty-two states have Right-to-Work laws that make unionization more difficult, and thus reduce union density. Lower union density in these states, can be partially attributed by lower worker demand for union representation, and by greater difficulty for unions to organize workers. These states tend to have lower wage rates, because the union *threat effect* is less evident in Right-to-Work states.

DATA ANALYSIS

Right-to-Work laws are defined as: "...*statutes enforced in 22 states, under the provisions of the Taft-Hartley Act, which prohibit trade unions from making membership or paying union dues or 'fees' a condition of employment, either before or after hire.*" (http://www.reference.com/search?q=right%20to%20work%20laws&r=d&db=web).

"*A Right-to-Work law secures the right of employees to decide for themselves whether or not to join or financially support a union. Employees who work in the railway or airline industries are not protected by a Right to Work law, and those who work on a federal enclave may not be.*" (http://www.nrtw.org/rtws.htm).

"*State laws can make it illegal for labor unions and employers to enter into contract that provide for a business to employ only union members in the jobs covered by the contract. A typical version of a Right-to-Work law says that no person may be denied employment, and employers may not be denied the right to employ any person, because of that person's membership or non-membership in any labor organization.*" (http://www.auburn.edu/~johnspm/gloss/right-to-work).

Deregulation of previously highly regulated industries, such as trucking and transportation (1979), airlines (1978), and telecommunications (1984), has had an important affect on wages, benefits, and working conditions. These business sectors had strong union representation as regulated industries, and since deregulation, the union presence has been significantly reduced or eliminated. Non-union enterprises developed as a direct result of deregulation, and the threat effect has been reduced. As an example, in 2002, union density in Right-to-Work states was 5.0%, as opposed to 12.3% in non-Right-to-Work states.

Deregulation has greatly reduced union strength, and union industry saturation. As a result, the average wages in these industries has declined, which has helped lower consumer prices. The new firms developed business models based on lower non-union labor costs and less restrictive work rules. For example, discount airlines such as Air Tran, Southwest Airline, and Jet Blue are non-union carriers, and their rates are lower than the unionized legacy airlines. The deregulated interstate trucking industry permitted more owner-operator drivers, and lower cost non-union trucking companies to operate. Another example is the break up of AT&T and deregulation of the telephone and communications industries. The start-up telecommunications companies developed their business models of lower consumer prices, partially based on non-union wages and less restrictive work rules.

Collective bargaining agreements between unions and employers in non-Right-to-Work states require employees to pay union dues or agency fees, as part of their employment with the unionized company. Employees pay dues or fees, between 1% to 5% of each represented employee's wages, and these monies fund the unions' business operations. Right-to-Work states require unions to represent *all* the employees equally and without bias, regardless if some workers choose not pay dues or fees. The non-dues paying union workers are known as _free riders_ because they enjoy full union benefits without paying their fair share of the unions operating expenses in terms of union dues or fees. Non-paying union members create extra financial and staffing burdens on unions, can cause discord within the union membership, and is a contributing factor to the reduction of the *threat effect* in Right-to-Work states. (Princeton University Industrial Relations. Non-Union Wages Rates and the Threat of Unionization. Working Paper No. 472. Farber, Henry. Princeton University. 2003).

In Right-to-Work states, a lower percentage of workers choose to join unions, and if they do join unions, often opt out of paying dues. Union leadership is against Right-to-Work laws, because the laws weaken organized labors bargaining power, organizing efforts, income sources, and political strength. Right-to-Work proponents feel that workers should have free choice to negotiate their wages and benefits independently of collective bargaining agreements, and therefore should not be required to pay fees for union representation. In addition, a large portion of the union dues paid by workers, are used to support union centric political causes, and workers may not wish to contribute to causes they do not support. Opponents argue that Right-to-Work laws permit workers to enjoy a *'free ride'*, because they benefit from union representation without requiring them to pay their fair share for the union's services.

The Economic Decline of the American Middle Class

The *"American Dream"* of middle class prosperity is slipping partly due to the decline in organized labor strength. Unions helped build the American middle class, by raising wages for large segments of the working population, increasing benefits, and improving pensions and health care. Following World War II, union membership was over 35% of the private sector workforce. The government created minimum wage and hour laws, and improved health and safety regulations. The real value of the minimum wage declined because of reduced government social policies and weaker labor laws. (Economic Policy Institute Briefing Paper. *A New Social Contract-Restoring Dignity and Balance to the Economy.* Briefing Paper #184. Kochan and Schulman, 2007).

In 1979, 25% of the workforce was unionized, and in 1990, that number dropped to only 16%. Union membership in 2006 was down to less than 7.4% of private sector workers and only 12% of all workers when you include government employees. (Bureau of Labor Statistics, 2007, www.bls.gov). Union membership rates continue to decline. The government sector is the only bright spot, and even this segment is declining. Union membership affects all workers, because non-union companies wishing to remain non-union raise wages and benefits to thwart unionization. Unions argue they give workers a collective voice in the workplace, and improve wages, benefits, and working conditions. Unions maintain they created the American middle class, increased economic prosperity while reducing poverty, and decreased the reliance government social services.

The middle class is struggling, and real wages are flat, and in some industries, declining. Between 2000 and 2006, productivity increased 20%, while real wages increased only 2%. Over 25% of workers earned wages below the poverty level in 2005. (Economic Policy Institute Briefing Paper. *Unions, the Economy, and the Employee Free Choice Act*. Briefing Paper #181. Shaiken, Harley. 2007).

"Amid this country's strong economic expansion, many Americans simply aren't feeling the benefits," Henry Paulson, President Bush's Treasury Secretary, admitted in August 2006. Paul Krugman agreed, stating that *"All indicators of the economic status of ordinary Americans—poverty rates, family incomes, the number of people without health insurance—show that most of us were worse off in 2005 than we were in 2000, and there's little reason to think that 2006 was much better."* (Economic Policy Institute Briefing Paper. *Unions, the Economy, and the Employee Free Choice Act*. Briefing Paper #181. Shaiken, Harley. 2007).

It needs to be noted that corporate profits are very high, while workers wages are low in comparison. Corporate profits increased from 7.0% in 2001, to 12.2% in 2006, measured as a share of national income, which is the highest increase since 1947. The Economist Magazine noted in the summer of 2006: *"Growth is fast, unemployment is low, and profits are fat...only one in four Americans believe the economy is in good shape. While firms' profits have soared, wages for the typical worker have barely budged."* (Economic Policy Institute Briefing Paper. *Unions, the Economy, and the Employee Free Choice Act*. Briefing Paper #181. Shaiken, Harley. 2007).

Happy workers are more motivated workers, and produce better products, with less absenteeism and lower employment turnover, which reduces employee-training costs, increases worker commitment, and improves quality. Henry Ford understood this concept when he voluntarily raised wages to five dollars per day in 1914, from the prevailing wage rate of two to three dollars per day, and reduced the workday to eight hours, down from the prevailing nine to ten hour workday. Worker productivity increased dramatically, Ford reduced the unit price per vehicle, and profits soared. *"A low wage business is always insecure,"* Ford commented. The five-dollar day *"was one of the finest cost-cutting moves we ever made."* (Economic Policy Institute Briefing Paper. *Unions, the Economy, and the Employee Free Choice Act.* Briefing Paper #181. Shaiken, Harley. 2007).

Employers need to view workers not just as hourly costs factors, but also as productive partners. A modern employer and progressive labor union, working together, and not as adversaries, can achieve higher productivity, and higher wages, with increased competitiveness and higher corporate profitability. A case in point is the comparison between Costco and Sam's Club (a Wal-Mart company). Both firms sell similar products to similar customers, and are very aggressive competitors. Costco's labor costs are about 40% higher than Sam's Club is. In 2005, Costco's operating profit per employee was $21,805, as compared to Sam's Club of $11,615, and Costco's sales per square foot was $866, compared to $525 for Sam's Club. Moreover, Costco's employee turnover rate was only 6%, as compared to 21% for Sam's Club. Productivity and unionization can be positively related. (Economic Policy Institute Briefing Paper. *Unions, the Economy, and the Employee Free Choice Act.* Briefing Paper #181. Shaiken, Harley. 2007).

The Role of Government and Economic Prosperity

One of the roles of government is to distribute economic prosperity to the workers who are both a major contributor and a major benefactor. Business and labor are mutually dependent on each other. A company that fails to be profitable because of out dated union work rules or unrealistic government labor policies, files for bankruptcy or closes shop. An empty factory or closed store does not need workers. Simply put, no employer, no employees! The American Dream, and thus the nation's 'American Dream' of economic prosperity are co-dependent on progressive and productive labor relations. Globalization, outsourcing, downsizing, the internet, and advancements in technology, and are very real threats to the American worker. '<u>Made in America</u>' has become a history lesson, and now might mean, at best, '<u>Maybe Partially Assembled in America</u>.' The only realistic economic alternative is a co-dependent management and labor liaison, with government acting as a helpful *"consigliore"* or counselor and advisor to both sides.

The twenty- first century worker is more family centric, and government, labor, and industry should play an active role supporting family friendly benefits. The 1993 Family Medical Leave Act (FMLA) is a good step in the direction of permitting workers to be with family members in times of need and retain their jobs. However, over half of American workers and over 75% of low wageworkers do not have paid medical leave benefits, and cannot afford to miss time from work. For these workers, it is no work, no pay, which puts pressure on workers to choose between family needs, and economic survival needs. When families do not have health insurance or retirees do not have money when they are unable to work, the taxpayers in terms of social services programs and government subsidies, ultimately pay for their care.

In a perfectly balanced world, health insurance and retirement benefit programs ought to be developed that are portable and flexible, and help those in greater need. *"'Health Care for America,' which would create a public insurance pool linked to Medicare to cover those not insured through an employer-provided plan. Employers would have a choice to either pay into the public fund or substitute their own equal or better health insurance for the public plan if they prefer. Employees would pay premiums to the public*

DATA ANALYSIS

plan and non-employees would be required to purchase coverage on an income-based scale." (Economic Policy Institute Briefing Paper. *A New Social Contract-Restoring Dignity and Balance to the Economy.* Briefing Paper #184. Kochan, Thomas and Schulman, Beth. February 2007).

The Earned Income Tax Credit is an example of a government policy that helps families. It complements the minimum wage in two ways. *"First, it further increases income without negative employment effects because it reduces (or eliminates) income taxes on earned wages rather than increasing the wages employers pay. Second, it is linked to family needs by being graduated for the number of people in one's household. Combining increases in the minimum wage with increases in the Earned Income Tax Credit would help working families achieve incomes that move them out of poverty and start them on the way to earning a decent family wage and moving up the economic ladder."* (Economic Policy Institute Briefing Paper. *A New Social Contract-Restoring Dignity and Balance to the Economy.* Briefing Paper #184. Kochan, Thomas and Schulman, Beth. February 2007).

Just as the nature of work has changed, so has the nature of the workers. Gone are the stereotypical days of the male breadwinner and the female homemaker. The new worker demographics include:

- Today three-fifths of women age 16 and over are in the paid labor force, as are 70% of mothers with children under 16 years of age.
- Only 21% of married families fit the old *male breadwinner* model with the husband in the labor force and the wife at home, compared to 56% in 1950.
- Single parents now account for 10% of all households, up from 8% in 1979.
- Wives have increased their working hours by one-third to one-half between 1979 and 2004. The largest increases (535 hours or just under three months) have come from

wives in middle-income families. As a result, middle-income families with children now work approximately 3,500 hours per year, close to the equivalent of two full time workers. This is an increase of about 18% since 1979.
- Increased earnings by wives since 1979 accounted for all of the growth in real family incomes for families in the bottom two-fifths of the labor force and for about 80% of the growth in middle-income families.
- More than 20% of households report being responsible for some or all of the care of elderly relatives, and these percentages are expected to double in the near future as the population ages.

(Economic Policy Institute Briefing Paper. A New Social Contract-Restoring Dignity and Balance to the Economy. Briefing Paper #184. Kochan, Thomas and Schulman, Beth. February 2007).

Job Training

Government plays a very active role in American prosperity, by developing economic initiatives, and labor policies that benefit American workers. The economy is becoming global, aided by the internet, and the job market is shifting to knowledge-based work. Local, state, and federal governments should institute macroeconomic policies to support long-term job creation, and to provide the tools to educate, train and support workers. Microeconomic policies, such as localized job creation requires the support of a wide range of education, employment, and labor initiatives. All who want to work should be able to find meaningful work, and the role of government, industry, and unions, is to provide the education, training, and career paths to find work consistent with industry and community needs. Job initiatives should support national economic growth policies.

At a time when job-training investment ought to be increased to meet the needs, the U.S. Department of Labor has actually *decreased* funding. In 2006, the funding was $5.2 billion, which equates to $35 per worker, a steady twenty year decline from $6.1 billion or $63 per worker since 1986. (Economic Policy Institute Briefing Paper. *A New Social Contract-Restoring Dignity and Balance to the Economy.* Briefing Paper #184. Kochan, Thomas; Schulman, Beth. 2007).

The United States is quickly shifting to a knowledge based economic structure. To be effective, labor policies should be synchronized with the requirements of private industry. Life long career training programs must use the combined resources of colleges, trade schools, local, state and federal governments, private industry, trade groups, with the active union involvement. Organized labor should adopt a pro-active approach to long-term job training programs, as a method to sustain union growth. It is in the best interest of labor unions to have their members productively employed. The better-trained workers earn higher wages. The higher unionized employees wages are, the larger percentage of union dues are collected. Labor unions benefit. They can reinvest in relevant industry training that meets or exceeds the needs of the modern employer. Simply put, trained workers are an investment in the future survival of labor unions.

Craft unions in the construction and building trades have a rich history of investing in worker training through apprenticeship programs. Other unions such as the United Auto Workers (UAW), and the Communications Workers of America (CWA), have job training and career development programs as part of their collective bargaining contracts. Employers assume when they employ skilled union workers, they are well trained and experienced and therefore productive employees with improved safety records. Unionized workers are cost effective relative to their skills. (Economic Policy Institute Briefing Paper. *A New Social Contract-Restoring Dignity and Balance to the Economy.* Briefing Paper #184. Kochan, Thomas and Schulman, Beth. February 2007).

◄ IS ORGANIZED LABOR A DECAYING BUSINESS MODEL?

Union Job Banks

The concept of Job Banks was developed during the 1984 contract negotiations, between the United Auto Workers (UAW) union and Ford, Chrysler, General Motors and parts maker subsidiary, Delphi. From the union perspective, the Job Banks was a method to save jobs, by making layoffs very expensive for the company. The UAW reasoned this would force the automakers to increase production and prevent outsourcing. Unneeded workers were assigned to the Job Banks, until their services were needed on the factory floor, or they retired. Even though the name might imply otherwise, the Job Banks did <u>not</u> provide education or training for new jobs. The Job Banks did <u>not</u> provide economic value to the automotive industry or parts suppliers. However, the Job Bank concept <u>did</u> increase expenses while demoralizing experience and talented workers.

Over half million manufacturing jobs were lost during the recession of the late 1970's and early 1980's, and the UAW wanted to protect the remaining union membership from additional layoffs due to downsizing, automation and technology. Conversely, the automakers wanted to increase productivity and enhance manufacturing flexibility, through improved technology and automation. The companies also needed to adjusted work rules, and have the ability to reduce factory shifts and production schedules in conjunction with sales needs and model changes. The Job Banks was a compromise.

The reality is that it has forced the U.S. auto industry to produce more vehicles, not because of dealer sales requirements, but because it is more cost effective to keep factories operating and to pay workers to produce something, rather than paying workers to sit idle and close factories. To sell these unwanted vehicles, the automakers forced dealers to take the vehicles, and then offered huge rebates, zero percentage interest, or other unprofitable incentives just to sell the products. The unintended consequence was to create a consumer sales mentality that people only wanted to buy vehicles offering huge incentives. When the incentives stopped, sales dropped steeply, and factories closed.

Paid Not To Work

On paper, the Job Banks appeared as a reasonable trade off between the UAW and the auto companies. In reality, it became the epitome of a good idea gone badly. The only requirements are that the union members, who have been placed in the Job Banks, show up at the Job Banks instead of the factory. The workers are not required to do any work. They often read, play cards, do crossword puzzles or sleep. *Remember, the workers were paid their full salaries, plus benefits, including seniority, to do absolutely nothing!*

Over 12,000 UAW autoworkers were paid <u>NOT</u> to work, at total potential four-year cost of over $4.1 billion dollars. The labor contracts signed in 2003 and ending in 2007 with the UAW specify the four-year caps the auto companies must pay into the Job Banks. For example, GM is spending over $2.1 billion, with Delphi contributing another $630 million; Ford and Ford subsidiaries payments are $944 million; while Daimler-Chrysler costs are $451 million, add another $50 million for UAW salaried workers, bringing their total to $501 million. The number of workers in the Job Banks is startling.

GM led the automotive group with 5,000 workers, followed by Delphi parts division with 4,000 workers, and Chrysler with 2,100 workers. Ford had the least, with 1,275 workers. (http://www.detnews.com/2005/autoinsider/0510/17/A01-351179.htm).

Delphi, the auto parts maker spun off from General Motors, has 36,000 U.S. employees, with about 12% or 4,000 workers in the Job Banks. *"Can we keep losing $400 million a year paying workers in the jobs bank, and $400 million a quarter on operations?"* Delphi Corporation, CEO Steve Miller said. *"No,*

IS ORGANIZED LABOR A DECAYING BUSINESS MODEL?

we cannot deal with that indefinitely. We simply cannot compete and cannot survive long-term unless we reduce our costs." (http://www.detnews.com/2005/autosinsider/0509/28/A01-330541.htm).

A report published in the Detroit News, "Cyber Survey" in October 2005, asked the following question: *"With thousands of laid off autoworkers costing the auto industry hundreds of millions of dollars for their jobs banks, is it time the auto industry shed itself of this program?"* The final vote was YES: 87.85%, and NO: 12.15%. (http://www.detnews.com/2005/autosinsider/0510/17/A01-351179.htm).

A majority of the workers dislike going to the Job Banks, and regard it as degrading, referring to it as 'rubber rooms', or 'being put out to pasture.' The original intent was to have workers gainfully employed, in a stand-by mode and ready to go to back to work. To be effective, the Job Banks must provide employee re-training to learn new skills, and therefore more useful to the company and themselves. Most of these workers are highly skilled, and have decades of experience. The reality has been very different from the intent. It is a sad waste of human talent, a huge brain drain with staggering financial costs, and a contributing factor to the U.S. auto industry decline.

The UAW agreed to close the Job Banks as part of the government bailout package.

No employer or industry can afford to pay a large group of workers to produce absolutely nothing. Obviously, going forward, this is not sustainable business model for an industry that is financially collapsing, and losing significant market share to more efficient Asian, Korean and other foreign automakers. American unionized automakers have systemic institutional inefficiencies, and will not survive, unless they make radical changes. A business or industry cannot continue to remain unprofitable for an indefinite period, before the simple laws of economics forces bankruptcy, consolidation, or closure.

The foreign carmakers, building cars in U.S. plants, generally are non-union, and therefore are not burdened with costly Job Banks, antiquated work rules, long-term health care, and pension obligations. As non-union employers, they are not subject to union work rules that intentionally increase employment, and protect the jobs of current employees, while actually decrease productivity. These companies remain largely non-union by paying the workers nearly comparable wages and benefits as UAW workers. The employers enjoy the benefits of being an at-will employer, with production and work force flexibility, and increased productivity at lower total labor costs.

Blue-Collar Blues

The decline in production of U.S. cars and light trucks has created large pools of unionized workers unemployed, temporary laid-off or in Job Bank programs. GM had about 12,000 workers in temporary laid-off status. The 2003 union contract, which expired in 2007, requires GM to pay 95% of the workers regular salary for 48 weeks, and after 48 weeks, the workers are placed in Job Banks, where they can earn $52,000 per year plus benefits. Partially because of slow sales, unprofitable manufacturing facilities, antiquated work rules, high health care and retiree liabilities, and compounded by a depressed economy, GM, Chrysler and other unionized U.S. car companies have closed or sold legendary product brands. The car companies and parts suppliers have received federal government bailout money and forced into bankruptcy reorganization. The net result is the collapse of the legacy auto industry, with the optimistic outlook of a new, lean, and green industry. The economic pain has not only created displaced workers, but has also created ripple effects of depressed local and state economies. The car companies and suppliers have offered unionized employees buyouts and other financial incentives, as a method to reduce labor costs. The unionized domestic auto manufacturers are faced with a paradigm shift in their business models and have few competitive alternatives other than federal bailout funding, bankruptcy reorganization, downsizing operations, outsourcing jobs, closing factories and reducing employment.

Union Dues and Per Capita Taxes

Labor unions collect dues from their membership and dues are a primary source of income. Unions may also have other sources of income from diversified investments, and may provide members additional services such as credit cards and mortgage lending. Union dues income pays for salaries, operating expenses, organizing, and political power, through contributions and active support. The local unions pay the national union, who pays the international union. The franchising system might be an analogy, where the local franchise store pays the national company a percentage of gross sales, or a per unit fee, for name recognition, business supplies, support services, and advertising contributions.

Union dues are primarily are used for the direct benefit of the membership, such as organizing activities, salaries, and administrative costs. Dues, which are essentially monthly membership fees, vary by union, by occupational classification within each union, or by salary or other methods, but range from 1% to 5% of gross income. Unions may or may not charge an initiation fee or joining fee. *"In 1997 members of the UAW paid 1.15 % of their monthly income in dues or the equivalent to two hours' pay. The UAW allocates 38 % of the dues to local union, 32 % to the national union's general fund, and 30 % to the strike fund. The local and national unions use these funds for union activities, for paying organizers and other staff members who take part in collective bargaining and hearing grievances. The strike fund supports union members during a walkout or a lockout, when they receive no pay. During contract negotiations, a large strike fund helps convince employers that the union is prepared to strike, thereby strength-*

DATA ANALYSIS

ening the union's bargaining power." (http://encarta.msn.com/text_761553112___0/Labor_Union.html).

For example, union dues for SEIU-UHW (Service Employees International Union-United Healthcare Workers) union are *"... 2% of base monthly pay, not including overtime. A full-time employee making $12 an hour would pay monthly dues of $41, and a full-time employee making $23 or more an hour would pay monthly dues of $82. Newly organized members do not pay dues until a contract is negotiated." (www.seiu-uhw.org/organizing/unionfaqs.html# How_ much_are_union_dues)*. Local 1199 of the Service Employees International Union, *"... members pay 2% of their monthly wages in dues. There is no initiation fee for newly organized members, and new members do not pay dues until they have voted to approve a contract and experience the benefits of membership."* (http://www.1199seiu.org/join/formingunion.cfm#Q6). The International Brotherhood of Electrical Workers Union, Local 45, states dues are *"$11.00 per month."* (http://ibew45.org/dues_benefits/dues_payment_info.html). National Education Association, representing teachers, whose members in 2003 spent an average of $443.00 annually for union dues. (http://educationchoice.blogspot.com/2006/11/teacher-spending-on-supplies-and-union.html).

Generally, union dues structures are based on the principle that the more you earn, the more dues you pay. Union dues can also be viewed as a union imposed tax on unionized employee wages, or as a monthly membership fee paid in return for the benefits and protection the union provides.

The point must be emphasized that union dues are the basic funding mechanisms for organized labor. There are wide variations in the union funding structures, including dues, initiation fees or joining fees, special assessment fees, used for example to build a strike fund, and per capita taxes or per member assessments.

Per capita taxes is a membership tax or assessment fee, or per head tax, imposed as a *"... per-head charge required to be paid* to the International Union on all monthly dues payments received by a Local Union during any given month." (http://www.seiu.org/olc/workshop/glossary.html). The AFL-CIO notes "...a per capita tax shall be paid upon the full paid-up membership of each affiliated national or international union, organizing committee and directly affiliated local union." (http://www.aflcio.org/aboutus/thisistheaflcio/constitution/art16.cfm).

For example, all union members affiliated with the AFL-CIO are required to pay a per capita tax that is factored into their normal union dues. A certain amount of the dues income is divided between the local union, national and international union, to be used for the benefit of the membership. The AFL-CIO Executive Council on August 07, 2007 at the Chicago convention issued the following statement about affiliated per capita taxes: *"Per capita taxes paid by the national and international unions of the AFL-CIO make up the AFL-CIO's principal income. This system of financing is predicated on principles of democratic participation, fairness and accuracy: The AFL-CIO Convention establishes the amount of the tax; larger affiliates pay a relatively larger overall share of the tax; and every affiliate obligates itself to report and pay on behalf of all individuals whose dues are subject to the tax. The AFL-CIO Constitution establishes a specific amount of per capita tax on each affiliate's full paid-up membership."* (http://www.aflcio.org/aboutus/thisistheaflcio/ecouncil/ec08072007k.cfm).

Full financial data, such as income, assets, expenses, officers' salaries, and union dues are public record, and reported to the U.S. Department of Labor (DOL). The Labor Management Reporting and Disclosure Act (LMRDA), in 2004, reported union dues of the largest labor organizations. Union dues variations range from a high of $830 per year for the IOUE (International Union of Operating Engineers), to a low of $210 per year for the Steelworkers Union. Building trades, such as electricians and laborers tend to have higher average dues than other unions, as do those that represent traditionally low wage and low skilled workers, such as hotel workers and building cleaners. Union dues have been increasing significantly, because of the higher costs of doing business, and as a reaction to specific events, such as replenishing strike funds or increased expenses for organizing or political activities. Unfortunately, dues are also raised to pay for higher officer salaries. For example, the president of the Operating Engineers earned $807,626 in 2004, in salary and allowances, making him the highest paid union official that year. (http://www.labornotes.org/node/908).

Average Union Dues in 2004 and Union Dues Growth from 2000 to 2004

Union Name	Average Annual Dues Paid per Member in 2004	Real Dues Growth from 2000 to 2004
National Education Association (NEA)	$281.00	4.3%
Service Employees International (SEIU)	$405.00	16.7%
United Food and Commercial Workers (UFCW)	$399.00	12.3%
American Federation of State, County, Municipal Employees (AFSCME)	$269.00	17.1%
International Brotherhood of Teamsters (IBT)	$490.00	18.6%

IS ORGANIZED LABOR A DECAYING BUSINESS MODEL?

Union	Dues	Growth
Union of Needletrades, Industrial & Textile Employees-Hotel Employees, Restaurant Employees (UNITE-HERE)	$380.00	4.8%
American Federation of Teachers (AFT)	$236.00	(6.4) %
Laborers' International Union of North America (LIUNA)	$647.00	(8.1) %
International Brotherhood of Electrical Workers (IBEW)	$688.00	4.6%
United Auto Workers (UAW)	$516.00	7.1%
International Association of Machinists (IAM)	$231.00	(15.9) %
Communications Workers of America (CWA)	$369.00	15.6%
United Steelworkers of America (USWA)	$210.00	(7.1) %
United Brotherhood of Carpenters (UBC)	$271.00	(16.4) %
International Union of Operating Engineers (IUOE)	$830.00	10.2%
TOTAL AVERAGES	**$377.00**	**(8.4) %**

(http://www.labornotes.org/node/908)

Union dues and real dues growth in 2004, the latest year data was collected, for the largest 15 unions, reveals the average annual dues were $ 377 with a <u>decline</u> of 8.4 % in real dues growth. This percentage loss of real dues income can be partly attributed to the decline in union membership, which also translates to loss of union power and political influence. *Once again, the point must be emphasized that union dues are the basic funding mechanisms for organized labor.*

Union Statistics

The Bureau of Labor Statistics notes that government sector employees have a unionization rate almost four times than private sector workers. Private sector growth rates have steadily declined, while government sector rates have essentially remained stable. Organized labor views most branches of government and most job classification below the managerial level as a growth segment. Politically and operationally, it is easier and less contentious to organize government workers than private sector employees. The argument is that the private sector must show a profit to shareholders and lenders, where as the government must only show their constituents effective programs administration and timely customer service. (http://www.unionfacts.com/states/).

Largest Labor Unions in the United States:

AFL-CIO

Auto Workers (UAW)

Carpenters (CJA)

Communications Workers (CWA)

Electrical Workers (IBEW)

Operating Engineers (IUOE)

Laborers (LIUNA)

Letter Carriers (NALC)

Machinists (IAM)

National Education Association (NEA)

Plumbers and Pipe Fitters (PPF)

Postal Mail Handlers Union (NPMHU)

Service Employees International Union (SEIU)

State, County & Municipal Employees (AFSCME)

Steelworkers (USWA)

Teachers (AFT)

Teamsters (IBT)

United Food & Commercial Workers (UFCW)

IS ORGANIZED LABOR A DECAYING BUSINESS MODEL?

UNITE HERE
(http://www.unionfacts.com/unions/)

Top 10 blue-collar jobs based on salary medians and expected growth by 2014:

Construction and Building Inspectors
ANNUAL PAY: $43,670
EXPECTED EMPLOYMENT GAIN: 18 percent to 26 percent

Waste and Wastewater Treatment Plant and System Operators
ANNUAL PAY: $34,960
EXPECTED EMPLOYMENT GAIN: 9 percent to 17 percent

Elevator Installers and Repairers
HOURLY PAY: $28.23
EXPECTED EMPLOYMENT GAIN: 9 percent to 17 percent

Subway and Streetcar Operators
HOURLY PAY: $23.70
EXPECTED EMPLOYMENT GAIN: 9 percent to 17 percent

Iron and Metal Workers
HOURLY PAY: $20.40
EXPECTED EMPLOYMENT GAIN: 9 percent to 17 percent

Electricians
HOURLY PAY: $20.33
EXPECTED EMPLOYMENT GAIN: 9 percent to 17 percent

Brick Masons, Block Masons, and Stonemasons
HOURLY PAY: $20.07
EXPECTED EMPLOYMENT GAIN: 9 percent to 17 percent

Plumbers, Pipe Layers, Pipe Fitters and Steamfitters
HOURLY PAY: $19.85
EXPECTED EMPLOYMENT GAIN: 9 percent to 17 percent

Heating, Air Conditioning and Refrigeration Mechanics and Installers
HOURLY PAY: $17.43
EXPECTED EMPLOYMENT GAIN: 18 percent to 26 percent

Carpenters
HOURLY PAY: $16.78
EXPECTED EMPLOYMENT GAIN: 9 percent to 17 percent
(Sources: Bureau of Labor Statistics www.bls.gov, and Career Builder web site: www.Careerbuilder.com).

Union Membership and Income Down

The AFL-CIO, with national headquarters in Washington, DC, is the largest and oldest union umbrella organization representing a major portion of all unionized workers. The general trend in recent years has seen a decline in union membership, and therefore a decline in revenue. As an example, membership in 2002 was 13,140,393, in 2005 union membership increased slightly to 13,696,392, and has declined to 9,875,234 in 2006. Total assets in 2002 were $98,783,070, in 2005 increased to $103,914,756, and has been reduced to $96,044,910 in 2006. Receipts in 2002 were $79,737,411, in 2005 increased to $189,887,090, and have diminished to $157,258,701 in 2006. Disbursements have closely mirrored receipts during the same years. (http://www.unionfacts.com/unions/unionFinances.cfm?id=106&year=2006)

Realizing that union membership numbers have been rapidly declining, and frustrated with the AFL-CIO's financial and political support of the Democratic Party, the Change to Win (CtW) organization in 2005, split from the AFL-CIO, taking with it seven of the more powerful and aggressive unions. This is a contributing factor to the decline in membership, money and to an extent political capital of the AFL-CIO.

The CtW business model and operating philosophy is to spend

IS ORGANIZED LABOR A DECAYING BUSINESS MODEL?

money and human resources on organizing the unorganized workers. Organizing is the backbone of the labor movement, and diversification of industries and job classification is the key to a well balance portfolio. Using this method of organizing and diversification, unions insulate themselves from economic or political failures of specific business sectors. Organized labor also may enjoy an upturn of a sector, such as unionizing government workers, when manufacturing industries are declining. A similar corporate analogy is to aggressively seek, nurture and service new clients, in various industries.

It should be noted that the larger the work force and the greater variation of industries and job classifications represented by a specific union or federation of unions, the greater economic and political power enjoyed by organized labor. The more voices, the louder the chorus, and the greater influence the union has when negotiating labor contracts with employers on behalf of their represented employees. Unions obtain a majority of their income from union dues, and therefore the business model is to organize as many workers, in as many industries as possible, to derive as much income as possible. The economic and political business model is to *organize or perish*.

The United Auto Workers Union (UAW) has been losing membership, because of the decline in U.S. auto industry and heavy manufacturing. The global marketplace has created a need for manufacturing industries to close legacy plants in the U.S. and open efficient operations in low-wage nations. It is cheaper to make it in China, and sell it in Chicago, than make it in Chicago. Foreign auto companies have been building cars in U.S. plants, primarily in low-wage states, with non-union workers, and aggressively selling the vehicles at very competitive prices. The non-union producer is not hampered with out dated work rules, expensive retirement obligations and antiquated facilities.

For example, the UAW saw a decline in membership from 638,722 in 2002, to a 2006 low of 538,444, a loss of over

100,000 dues paying union members. If you viewed each union member as a separate account worth $516.00 annual average dues, then the loss of 100,000 accounts amounts to $51,600,000.00 business decline. From a purely income perspective, how long can a business or industry sustain such huge losses and remain a viable business? The UAW fate is directly tied to the U.S. legacy carmakers declining fate, and therefore not a long term sustainable business model.

The International Brotherhood of Teamsters (IBT) has actually enjoyed an increase of over 48,500 union members from 2002 to 2006. The average annual dues per member are $490, which represents $23,765,000 business increase during those years. The Teamsters represents workers in their core industries, such as transportation, trucking and warehousing. The union has diversified to represent workers in other industries, such as airlines, automotive and aerospace, chemical industries, bakery, brewery and soft drinks, the building and construction trades, plus the motion pictures and entertainment industries. The IBT represents diversified job classifications including airline pilots, mechanics, flight attendants, parking attendants and workers at United Parcel Service, Disney Land and Disney World employees. The IBT has a strong presence representing white-collar and blue-collar workers, technicians, and degreed professional public sector employees, such as nurses, police, corrections, court systems, and attorneys. The IBT total assets from 2002 to 2006 have increased from $85,119,996 to $177,767,292, and total receipts increased from $119,781,360 in 2002 to $178,535,878 in 2006. With a wide and diversified membership base, and an increase in assets and receipts, the Teamsters union represents a formidable economic and political force. (http://www. unionfacts.com/unions/unionFinances. cfm?id=93&year=2006).

The American Federation of State, County & Municipal Employees (AFSCME), represents government employees, has enjoyed steady membership growth from 2002 to 2006. From

IS ORGANIZED LABOR A DECAYING BUSINESS MODEL?

2002 though 2004, the membership was steady at 1,350,000. In 2005, this increased to 1,459,511, and in 2006, membership increased to 1,470,095. The numbers show that from 2004 to 2006 there were 120,000 new members, at an average union dues rate of $269 per member, equals a dues income increase of $32, 280,000, in two years.

Total assets showed a comfortable increase from $45,986,335 in 2002, to a 2006 total of $55,840,126. The Department of Labor, Office of Labor Management Standards, LM2 filings, shows the union has 631 employees, with 208 employees earning over $75,000 annually. AFSCME focus on local government employees and health care workers. (Source: Department of Labor, Office of Labor Management Standards, LM2 filings, and http://www.unionfacts.com/unions/unionProfile.cfm?id=289).

The International Association of Machinist and Aerospace Workers (IAM), an AFL-CIO trade union representing workers in over 200 industries, has suffered a decline in dues paying union membership, from 673,095 in 2002 to 646,933 in 2006. This is a decline of 26,162 paid members at an annual average of $231 dues per member, equals a $6,043,422 net dues revenue loss from 2002 to 2006. This is a significant revenue and membership loss, and indicates a decline in this trade, partly because of technology, globalization, and outsourcing. The IAM has 408 employees. (http://www. unionfacts.com/unions/unionProfile. cfm?id=107).

The IAM union has 212 decertification petitions filed. A decertification petition is an election request filed with the National Labor Relations Board by the represented union employees, asking the NLRB to end the union's rights as the employee's exclusive bargaining agent, and indicates the employees are unhappy with the union's performance. The results of the election determine if the union ceases to represent the employees or if the union still prevails as the exclusive bargaining agent. Employees may choose another union through the card check or election process to represent them, or may choose to become non-union shop. (http://www.unionfacts.com/glossary.cfm).

The Hotel Employees and Restaurant Employees (HERE) union, which represents hotel and restaurant workers, has maintained an average of 250,000 dues paying members from 2002 through 2004. Large hotel chains such as Hyatt, Hilton, Walt Disney World, and Las Vegas casinos Harrah's, Caesars, contract with HERE for hospitality workers. In 2004 HERE merged with the Union of Needletrades, Industrial, and Textile Employees (UNITE), to form UNITE-HERE. In 2005, the union left the AFL-CIO federation and joined the Change to Win coalition (CtW).

The combined union UNITE-HERE has 458,901 members in 2006, with total assets of $256,262,784, and 527 employees. There are 202 Decertification Petitions filed, with the National Labor Relations Board. There are also 1,873 Unfair Labor Practices (ULP) cases filed since 2000. *"The NLRB investigates instances of union violations of the National Labor Relations Act and other labor laws. Unfair Labor Practices include instances of bad faith bargaining, excessive dues, violence, threats, and many other violations."* (http://www.unionfacts.com/unions/unionProfile.cfm?id=511#UnfairLabor). (Source: National Labor Relations Board's Case Activity Tracker (CATS) system).

Labor unions earn a major portion of their income directly from dues paying members, and the trend in the labor movement has witnessed a general decline in membership. Selected unions have chosen mergers as an economic survival business model. Other unions have been fortunate to expand from their original core competencies and diversified into growth industries and job classifications. Unions representing local, state, and federal government workers have enjoyed an increase in membership because of increased unionization in the public sector.

CHAPTER 5

Globalization of Union Jobs

Globalization and the Unionized Blue-Collar Worker

The unionized blue-collar worker helped build the American middle class. It is becoming clear that unionized blue-collar prosperity is declining rapidly. Globalization, downsizing, outsourcing, and technology are all valid reasons for the decline of the labor movement. Some of the blame must rest with the labor unions. Unions have failed to change with the times. Union survival depends on adapting to the needs of business.

An example is the Newark, Delaware Chrysler plant that is schedule for closure. Many employees have spent their entire working lives at this plant, and the hope of finding employment that provides similar salaries and benefits is marginal at best. The plant has suffered from the same global dynamics that is affecting the industry. Older plants are inefficient to operate, and make products that fail to meet the consumer needs. This coupled with expensive unionized workers, with high retirement and high health care costs, using labor-intensive work rules designed to protect union jobs, and not increase productivity, is a recipe for economic disaster.

IS ORGANIZED LABOR A DECAYING BUSINESS MODEL?

It is a business model that is unsustainable, when compared to the costs of producing the product globally. Simply put, it is cheaper to make American cars in China, than Delaware, and then ship the cars back to U.S. markets. In this scenario, the U.S. automakers, and other industries, must become globally competitive, if they are to survive in the world markets. Organized labor must realize that the old ways of doing business are over, and accept that globalization is the new economic world order. Failure to accept this reality will lead to a labor movement that will largely become irrelevant. One thing is certain, if you continue do business as usual, it usually means you are out of business.

From 1985 to 2000, the only state to loose manufacturing output was Delaware. Manufacturers have invested heavily in labor savings technology, which requires fewer workers. Robotics and computers now do the work that formally required many workers on the factory line. Just in time deliveries, and pre-assembled components, have also reduced the need for manufacturing workers, improved production practices and in the long term, are more cost effective, and consequently more globally competitive. The global economy has created opportunities for manufactures to build plants in countries with less regulations and lower wages, and as a result, forced closures of U.S. facilities.

The reality is that from 1990 to 2001, in Delaware 13,900 manufacturing jobs were lost. Nationally, between 1998 and 2005, over 3.4 million manufacturing jobs were lost, and 40,423 manufacturing plants closed between 1999 and 2004. There is every expectation that the declines will continue, as the costs of doing business in emerging markets is significantly less than domestically.

Alan Tonelson, research fellow at the U.S. Business and Industry Council said, *"It's clear that the future of blue-collar employment not only in Delaware but throughout the United States is looking increasingly grim. The nation's leaders are allowing foreign nations to stack the deck when it comes to 'free trade,' putting U.S. industry at a competitive disadvantage ... America's leadership to must impose emergency tariffs on some imports until other nations stop subsidies that give them much of their advantage over U.S. manufacturers... It creates a hidden subsidy for foreign products coming into the U.S., and it imposes a hidden tax on U.S. products sent into foreign markets."* (http://www.delawareonline.com/apps/pbcs.dll/article?AID=/20070218/BUSINESS/302180008/1003).

Globalization and manufacturing technology have contributed to the decline in unionized blue-collar employment. One robot can do the work of many skilled workers. Robots do not go to 'Union Job Banks' and paid to do nothing. Robots are not unionized, do not ask for wage or benefit increase, do not require long-term health care and never go on strike. Robots are the perfect employee. Robots are just re-programmed to do another job function.

Manufacturing technology and globalization are economic realities. It is more cost effective for companies to have the work done in low wage nations, transported and sold to high wage nations, than produced domestically. The U.S. government gave foreign automakers tax incentives, to build U.S. factories, usually in lower wage states. The foreign automakers created blue-collar and white-collar jobs in states with high unemployment, improving the prevailing area wages, and raising the local standards of living. The plants are staffed with younger, non-union, less costly workers, and as a result the retirement and health care liabilities for the employers are less expensive. The legacy U.S. automakers and related industries, are usually staffed with unionized, older, higher paid workers, and require larger employer expenditures for benefits, such as retirement and health care.

Tonelson said, *"Assuming that the global trade situation doesn't change dramatically soon, I would argue that the very best that factories could hope for is a very significant downsizing... There is much more to come... Companies have to be more involved, they have to be more flexible. Unions have to realize they are not going to get all things. You just can't pay workers for doing nothing in the global competitive environment."* (http://www.delawareonline.com/apps/pbcs.dll/article?AID=/20070218/BUSINESS/302180008/1003).

The key to unionized blue-collar prosperity is education and training directly related to the current and future needs of employers. The alternative is a major decline in the unionized blue-collar middle class, resulting in economic drains for the nation. The <u>Working Poor Families Project</u>, in 2004, found that 25% of working families earn wages below $36,784 in 2002. Community colleges, state schools, union and employer sponsored career-training programs are needed. Not all careers may require a college education. Trade specific training schools can meet the demands of employers. For example, as manufacturing declines, other high tech fields expand. The point is that resources must be invested wisely, with direct career objectives, which meet current and projected employment needs, and workers career goals. All parties must equally benefit. (http://www. delawareonline.com/apps/pbcs.dll/article?AID= /20070218/BUSINESS/302180008/1003).

Lifetime employment, if it ever really existed in the United States, is an outdated concept and does not fit in with a fast changing global environment. Employers are faced with a talent war for the best workers they can afford. Employees want to feel they are making a difference. The better employers create workplace cultures based on employee satisfaction and career enhancement. The talent wars have created friendlier work environments, such as employee fitness centers, day care centers, helping families balance work and family time, offering time off to care for children or an elderly parent, and caring bosses willing to give workers flexible time schedules, to reduce commuting stress. Happy workers are productive workers and the employer benefits. (http://tech.groups.yahoo. com/group/TechsUnite/message/25991).

GLOBALIZATION OF UNION JOBS

Globalization Defined

The tragic death of Princess Diana explains globalization, through the following whimsical example, attributed to an anonymous source:

Let us examine the reasons:

An English princess, with an Egyptian boyfriend, crashes in a French tunnel, driving a German car, with a Dutch engine, driven by a Belgian, who was drunk on Scottish whiskey, followed closely by Italian Paparazzi, on Japanese motorcycles. An American doctor, using Brazilian medicines, treated her. An American is sending this message, using Microsoft technology, developed by an America citizen named Bill Gates. You may be reading this on a computer, that use Taiwanese chips, and a Korean monitor, assembled by Bangladeshi workers, in a Singapore plant, transported by Indian lorry-drivers, hijacked by Indonesians, and trucked to the US by Mexicans truckers, under NAFTA regulations, and shipped to a Wal-Mart near you somewhere in America.

Downsizing and Corporate Culture

Downsizing can be defined as a *"a set of organizational activities undertaken on the part of management of an organization and designed to improve organizational efficiency, productivity, and/or competitiveness"*. (http://www.pamij.com/hickok.html). In other words, for various reasons, management has chosen to reduce the workforce in the organization. The reality can be painful for the downsized employees and reduce morale for the surviving workers. Downsizing the workforce for the immediate goal of saving money is often a very short sighted and disruptive business model. Companies soon discover they have to hire outside contractors, usually at a higher cost per labor-hour, to do the work of the former downsized workers, and usually spend more than they may have saved. Management also suffers from a brain drain, when it loses the long-term employees who have the technical skills and understand the corporate culture. When business improves, it is often difficult to quickly bring the company up to speed, and to intellectual re-tool the corporate culture. In essence, hasty downsizing produces negative results and is counter productive to success.

There are advances in technology and economic global competitive realities that reduce the power of the unionized rank-and-file worker, and increase the pressure of management to increase corporate profitability. This has fundamentally changed the nature of work. No longer does a unionized blue-collar or white-collar employee expect to spend their entire working lives with one employer, and retire with a gold watch and a small pension for a lifetime of service. Global competition has forever changed the employment business model. Workers overseas are increasing more capable of producing equivalent goods and services at lower cost, and with equal or greater productivity.

Employees and employers must become competitive in the world markets. There are no employment entitlements, as there also are no employer entitlements to stay in business. _Proactive downsizing_ is carefully planned, less disruptive and usually part of a larger business model, such as a change in the market place, or a technological change in the types of goods and services sold. _Reactive downsizing_ because of an immediate cost cutting need is very disruptive to the employees, the community and the industry. An example is the auto industry downsizing, through layoffs and buyouts of thousands of employees, caused by poor auto sales, due partially to the industries failure to understand the changing market, and recognize the threat of increased foreign competition.

Downsizing methods can be culturally disruptive, forceful, and painful. An example might be a decision to eliminate the third shift at the factory, or in the extreme, to close the entire factory. A culturally kinder downsizing approach might be offering the employees on the third shift various choices, to include downsizing through attrition, early retirement, or career re-training, and to re-tool the factory to make other products. Various ways to downsize can be culturally more, or less disruptive. The methods may include, last hired, first fired, and explaining the options openly with the employees and soliciting feedback, or secretively terminating selected workers, shifts, or divisions. A best-case scenario and less disruptive method is to give workers advanced notice, so they can prepare, and have time to look for other jobs. A worse case and very disruptive scenario is to fire people on Friday at 5 pm, with no notice. This method demoralizes the surviving employees, resulting in low morale, mistrust, and reduced productivity.

Culture Reinforcing and Culture Destabilizing Downsizing Practice

CULTURE REINFORCING:

This is less disruptive, has more individual control, and likely to create *less* pain.

- Voluntary reductions, such as attrition, buyouts, job sharing.
- Advance notice, allows time to prepare, look for other job.
- Shared pain. For example, cuts across all levels-each department reduces staff.
- Explicit criteria for "who stays, who goes." Often *'last hired-first fired.'*
- Transition assistance. Morale is greatly improved.

CULTURE DESTABILIZING:

This is more disruptive, less individual control, and likely to create *more* pain.

- Involuntary reductions, such as layoffs or reduced work hours.
- Sudden termination. For example, fired on Friday at 5 pm, with no warning.

- Winners/losers. For example, executives get bonuses while cutting other jobs.
- Criteria are secret. Workers not told basis for downsizing.
- Little or no assistance for those who depart voluntarily or survivors. (http://www.pamij.com/hickok.html)

Employers should choose carefully. Poor termination methods can result in legal action, huge negative publicity, a drop in stock value, customers, and clients defecting to the competition, or a combination of adverse effects. Downsizing handle well, can create a new business model and change the corporate culture. The positive effects may include a highly competitive global business, with improved financial performance, and more engaged workers, who embrace the values of the improved company. *"The successful companies…also engaged in organizational redesign and systematic efforts at quality improvement…and engaged in downsizing as a purposeful and proactive strategy."* (http://www.pamij.com/hickok.html).

Outsourcing Union Jobs

Outsourcing, also known as sub-contracting, and obtaining wage concessions are economic business realities that concern white-collar and blue-collar workers alike. A manufacturing company, for example, may find it is more cost effective to outsource or sub-contract to an outside company, in the U.S. or abroad, that specializes in payroll and employee benefits, than do the work in house. Unionized blue-collar workers in the textile and manufacturing industries in strong unionized states have found their jobs sent to low wage nations, or low wage states in the United States. High tech white-collar workers such as software engineers have found their jobs outsourced. The bottom line for companies is to produce the best products for the lowest cost, consistent with quantity and quality. Business stakeholders are not concerned if the production facility, or call center is in Indonesia, India, or Indiana.

GLOBALIZATION OF UNION JOBS

Unionized employers may run into contractual conflicts when they attempt to outsource or sub-contract, if their collective bargaining agreement prohibits or limits this practice. Outsourcing has a direct effect on employees, in terms of income and job security, and can be disruptive and reduce morale. The unionized employer generally has a contractual duty to bargain or negotiate in good faith. *"A rare exception to the obligation to bargain regarding the decision to outsource may be made when the employer can show that the purpose of outsourcing turns 'not on labor costs but on a significant change in the nature and direction' of the company's business. Once a union represents a group of employees, the employer...is required to 'bargain collectively with the representative of its employees with respect to the terms and conditions of employment.'"* (Outsourcing and the Duty to Bargain, Snell & Wilmer, L.L.P).

Historically, the business model required manufacturing facilities located near sources of raw materials and transportation systems. Labor located near the factories, and towns and cities grew based on these employments centers. Fast forward to the late twentieth century, when advances in transportation, and telecommunications, and the Internet, changed the nature of work. Businesses are always searching for a lower cost and better way to conduct business. The modern business model no longer requires workers to be close to their workplace. With improvements in transportation and communications systems, it is often more profitable to have a product made in one location where wages and raw materials cost less and shipped to the buyers market, where wages and raw materials cost more. Unions can influence the outsourcing decision by influencing labor costs and work rules. In other words, to keep a major employer or industry locally, unions may be willing to reduces wages or loosen work rules.

◄ IS ORGANIZED LABOR A DECAYING BUSINESS MODEL?

Transformation of the Labor Market to Outsourcing Model ───

Outsourcing a factory or industry to a lower labor cost country or a lower labor cost state within the U.S., should <u>not</u> be based on the cost of labor alone. It is a complex process. Businesses do not operate in a vacuum, and decisions <u>must</u> be based on multiple factors. For example, stakeholders must consider political conflicts and corruption, crime, civilian unrest, transportation, taxes, quality, education, and availability of the local labor market. Other issues to consider include availability and quality of public utilities, such as water and electric, local infrastructure items such as roads, railroads or shipping channels, market access, raw materials availability, in addition to environmental issues, investment lending, financial security, and banking considerations. If these factors are within acceptable parameters, then outsourcing might make economic and business sense.

'<u>Union Made in America</u>' has become too costly, given global competition. Labor unions understand the needs of the workers, but few unions understand and accept the needs of business. The reality is the old ways of doing business do not work in the new global market place. Labor unions need to become a value added partner with business, and not an adversary to economic survival. The *'labor unions'* versus *'management'* mindset will lead to labor without a place to work, because management has moved the industry to a lower cost environment.

Downsizing and cutback are necessary when business conditions require these actions. Globalization is another method to help industries compete. The automotive industry is case in point. Work rules that may have been prudent in a different era, are contributing factors helping to make the industry unprofitable. It does <u>not</u> make economic sense for an industry to have *'Job Banks'*, and pay 12,000 workers <u>not</u> to work.

Dennis Martire is mid-Atlantic vice president and regional manager of the Laborers' International Union of North America

◄ 70

(LIUNA). The union represents some 40,000-construction laborers and other workers from Pennsylvania to North Carolina. He summed up labor and management needs succinctly, saying, "There are plenty of corporations earning unjustified windfall profits. There are also plenty of workers employed by union firms with thin profit margins. Demanding that companies in highly competitive markets retain unreliable workers, honor antiquated jurisdiction and work rules, and pay wages and benefits fully twice what their nonunion competitors pay is a recipe for disaster...When union contractors have no work, our members have no jobs. ...If unions are going to survive and prosper in the 21st century, we still need to meet the needs of workers, but we also need to find a way to serve important business needs... We can no longer simply demand that business adapt to our needs. We need to adapt to the needs of business..." (http://www.virginiaclassifieds.com/biz/virginiabusiness/magazine/ yr2006/dec06/ideas.shtml).

Outsourcing is a contributing factor to the decline of organized labor, is expected to increase, and is not limited to blue-collar workers. Educated, white-collar professional workers are experiencing major decrease in jobs, income, and health care benefits due to outsourcing. James Hoffa, president of the International Brotherhood of Teamsters, (IBT) which represents workers from airline pilots to zookeepers, said, "The 40-hour work week is under attack. The right to organize is under attack. We are fighting for retirement security. Fifty million Americans are without health care. And real wages are falling." (http://www.cioinsight.com/print_article2/0,1217,a=159450,00.asp).

Advocates of outsourcing consider it an extension of globalization, and site the need for employers to seek the best workers at the lowest costs, consistent with the technical skills and education levels needed to perform the business function. Supporters feel that U.S. businesses benefit by opening up international markets for their goods and services, while foreign workers enjoy greater economic opportunities. Given the reliance on technology, educated, skilled, and professional employees, such as engineers and technology workers will be in great demand.

Opponents argue the cost savings will be temporary, since these workers will become more expensive, as their skills increase and the demand for their talent increases. Outsourcing, opponents argue, is a wage race to the bottom, by forcing wages down. It is difficult for the U.S. worker to compete against cheaper foreign labor. For example, a talented software engineer in India may earn $10,000 yearly; where as the same person may earn $100,000 yearly in Indiana. Obviously, the Indian engineer is more cost effective, and will increase the companies' bottom line. Any loss in productivity can be improved by hiring two or three extra Indian engineers to help meet needs. It is virtually impossible on this basis, for the Indiana worker to compete with his Indian counterpart. (http://www.handsonnetwork.org/vca/employment-faqs/).

<u>Outsourcing</u> or sub contracting is the business process of taking work, such as payroll or software development to another company, either abroad or with in the U.S. Depending on the businesses core competencies, it is frequently more cost effective to contract out specific services, than do the work in house. <u>Offshoring</u> is the business process of moving work outside of the United States, to take advantage of other nation's lower wages, favorable tax structures, raw materials, or other business benefits.

Offshoring Jobs

The Progressive Policy Institute estimated that around 840,000 manufacturing jobs have been lost since the beginning of 2001 due to increased imports, and decreased export, and around 300,000 service jobs have been lost during this period. Forrester Research estimates that 3.4 million jobs, paying above $28,580 will be offshored by 2015. Higher wage U.S. jobs, including unionized jobs, will be moved to lower wage non-union nations. (*Understanding the Offshoring Challenge*. www.piponline.org).

GLOBALIZATION OF UNION JOBS

U.S. employers will move about 3.3 million white-collar service jobs and $136 billion in wages overseas in the next 15 years, up from $4 billion in 2000. (http://www.aflcio.org/aboutus/thisistheaflcio/publications/magazine/0903_amjobs.cfm).

Due to the competitive pressures of offshoring, American companies, both large and small, are reducing production capacity, consolidating, and filing for bankruptcy protection, or going out of business. They are forced to reduce or terminate some or all of their labor force, because they are unable to compete with lower cost non-union competitors. It is almost impossible for American businesses to compete with low wage nations. American retailers, such as Wal-Mart, are major buyers of foreign made goods. The ironic twist is that American consumers are happy to buy the lower cost foreign made products. On one hand American consumers save money buying low cost foreign products, and on the other hand, these products are closing American companies and costing American jobs.

Technology, such as Voice over Internet Protocol (VoIP), and the Internet, has made Bangalore, India as functionally close as Baltimore, Maryland has. Companies can do business with clients from any part of the globe, using English educated, well-trained employees at vastly reduced cost. Low wage nations have encouraged offshoring and developed the infrastructure needed for business to be conducted globally and almost seamlessly. The bottom line is it can make business sense for companies to offshore, as an economically viable alternative, to paying higher unionized wages.

"With NAFTA, the World Trade Organization and other trade deals of the last decade, American corporations are now tapping into a global supply of workers who can be trained to do everything from design to production, maintenance to marketing... While these workers become more productive, their pay doesn't rise, because in many of these countries, to be a labor organizer means you risk winding up in a ditch with a bullet in your head," says Jeff

Faux, economist and founding president of the Economic Policy Institute. American jobs offshored usually stay offshore. "*As long as employers can take advantage of much lower labor costs in other countries, there's no compelling reason to bring back many of these well-paying jobs... Policymakers seem to be at a loss as to what to do about this problem... To retain and create jobs, there have to be policy changes,*" said Ron Hira, assistant professor of public policy at Rochester Institute of Technology. (http://www.aflcio.org/aboutus/thisistheaflcio/publications/magazine/0903_amjobs.cfm)

Depending on your perspective, offshoring can be a benefit to business or a detriment to labor unions. Offshoring tends to lower prices of goods and services, increases competition, and reduce domestic production. Wall Street loves offshoring because it lowers labor costs, thus increasing business profits. Main Street and labor unions view offshoring with skepticism. An intended consequence of offshoring is to lower union and non-union wages, by forcing workers to compete with non-union low wage nations, thus encouraging a wage race to the bottom. When work is offshored, it increases job losses in local communities. It is impossible for a worker in Chicago to compete with a worker in China. It is very difficult for unions to justify higher wages, increased benefits, and antiquated work rules, when the employer can simply move the factory or call center offshore.

Interestingly, India has become comparatively expensive to offshore jobs. Other nations are competing for the business. Eastern European nations, such as Romania, Poland and the Czech Republic, and China, Malaysia, South Africa, Sri Lanka, Costa Rica and Ghana, have well educated workers, who speak English, French, Spanish and other languages, and are willing to work for lower wages and little benefits.

For example, GE Capital plans to increase their Indian employment to 20,000 workers, and Oracle plans on employing over 6,000 more people in India. Metropolitan Life Insurance has outsourced a major portion of its claims processing to offshore firms in Ghana, Mexico, China, and the Caribbean. Private and government sectors both utilize offshoring. New York City processes parking tickets in Ghana, and the World Bank performs most of its back office work in India. European companies utilize offshoring as cost effective business models. British Airways has 2,400 workers in India who handle passenger accounting, and British bank HSBC has 5,000 workers in Malaysia handling business processing. (*Understanding the Offshoring Challenge.* www.piponline.org).

New Jersey outsourced information and administrative functions for the state run welfare and food stamp benefits programs to India and Mexico. New Jersey callers were directed, for account information and assistance to press 'one for English', press 'two for Spanish'. The calls were routed to India or Mexico, and operators were able to process client claims. Call center workers used 'Americanized' names, and had full access to all client records, including Social Security numbers, date of birth, and income information.

The good jobs in America are being offshored to low wage non-union nations, while low wage jobs in America keep growing. The Department of Labor estimates that by 2010, 30% of American workers will earn less than poverty wages. Nearly 25% of American workers work in low wage service type jobs, such as office cleaning, nursing home and child care workers, food preparation and call centers. Many of these workers are African American or immigrants, and over 60% are female. The hourly pay to keep a family of four at the poverty level is $8.85, according to the U.S. government, and many of these workers earn the minimum wage, with little or no benefits. Disposable workers are low skilled workers doing jobs others do not want. As high skilled jobs are sent to low wage nations, low skilled jobs will become common in America. (http://www.aflcio.org/aboutus/thisistheaflcio/publications/magazine/0903_amjobs.cfm).

Offshoring threatens the American middle class by moving middle class jobs and middle class wages, to lower wage non-union nations. The African American middle class workers have suffered the most because of the loss of manufacturing jobs, with unemployment rates twice that of whites. Domestically, middle class jobs *decreased* by 157,600 from 1999 to 2002. During the same period, lower wage, service type jobs *increased* by 666,000 jobs, and higher wage, *knowledge type* jobs increased by 820,000. (*Understanding the Offshoring Challenge*. www.piponline.org).

Middle class job such as manufacturing, are the jobs that fit well with the offshoring business model. They also represent a large segment of union membership base. When you reduce the union workforce by offshoring their jobs, you reduce the union strength. Offshoring is a contributing factor to the decline of organized labor.

Privatization of Public Service

Privatization is defined as…"*The conversion of a public enterprise to a private enterprise. To change an industry or business, from governmental or public ownership or control to private enterprise. The transfer of ownership from the public sector to the private sector*" (http://dictionary.reference.com/browse/privatization).

Privatization of government services for the public good is neither good nor evil. There is no evidence that government deliveries of government social services are any more or less effective than the private delivery of government social services, through a for-profit or non-profit company. The success depends on the effectiveness of the customer services delivered, the financial and public accountability, and the quality of the services. The public is not concerned if the state, or a private company pays the representative on the other side of the counter, as long as the quality of services was satisfactory and courteous. The goals are to reduce delivery costs, while improving quality and quantity of service.

GLOBALIZATION OF UNION JOBS

Privatization of public services does reduce the number of unionized government employees. Arrangements are often made to transfer the former unionized employees to other government agencies. From the private sector viewpoint, it is very costly to loose the brain trust gained from years of knowledge and skills, and it is often beneficial and cost effective to keep the better government workers doing the same job for the private company. This is particularly true if the government services are specific or technical and not readily available in sufficient quantity or quality in the private sector. As an example, the government usually employs state welfare caseworkers, and if transferred to a private company, it would be beneficial to retain the skilled employees, since there may be a scarcity of highly skilled private sector welfare caseworkers seeking new employment.

There is a trend in government to provide enhanced services at lower cost. The Government Management Reform Act of 1994 (P.L. 103-356) states: *"To be successful in the future, government must, like the private sector, adopt modern management methods, utilize meaningful program performance measures, increase workforce incentives and flexibility without sacrificing accountability, and provide for humane downsizing opportunities and harness computers and other technology to strengthen service delivery."* (http://www.urban.org/publications/407023.html).

Both for-profit and non-profit companies have benefited by contracting service to various government entities. The 1966 welfare reform legislation has permitted states to privatize public social services. Massachusetts has allowed private companies to compete with state agencies to operate their 'One-Stop Career Centers' as part of the workforce development. The federal child support legislation encourages states to employ private contractors to locate parents who owe child support, provide accounting and enforcement of child support payments. Virginia and Georgia have privatized the entire child welfare system and private contractors manage full caseloads. There are several productivity reasons that private contractors succeed where government does not: contractors can add or reduce employees as needed to meet flexible work demands; they can invest heavily in better technology and computers as needed, and can pay incentive bonus for aggressive collections. *"Before the new welfare law, moving people from welfare to work was the domain of nonprofit organizations and three relatively small businesses. Now, some large companies see a potentially multibillion-dollar industry that could run entire welfare programs for states and counties."* (http://www.urban.org/publications/407023.html).

Does privatization save money and provide better public service? For Rudy Giuliani, as the mayor of New York City, the answer was "Yes." City services had fallen into decay, and Mayor Giuliani employed the private sector to improve daily city services and save taxpayers money. He sold city assets including gas stations, luxury hotels, parking garages, residential housing, radio, and TV stations, and the Coliseum exhibition center. The sales generated cash and reduced the cities financial liabilities. He instituted competitive bidding for city services such as meter reading, fleet management, and school custodial services. Privatization was the basis for fixing a dysfunctional city.

Union leadership is usually opposed to privatization, because they are concerned about job losses. Union opposition can derail privatization efforts, and therefore successful privatization must include organized labors support. Unions must accept that public services privatization can work. Certain New York City services were not possible to privatize, such as the hospital and prison systems. Mr. Giuliani summarized his accomplishments, *"We now have a broad array of privatization programs that impact nearly every aspect of the city government. We divested ourselves of businesses that... belong in the private sector. Now these properties generate tax revenues and private-sector jobs."* (Privatization Bears Fruit in the Big Apple. www.mackinac.org).

Mayor Giuliani proposed 82 privatization initiatives, of which

66 succeeded. New York City reduced cost by $6 billion and 23 different taxes were eliminated or reduced, proving the city could be governed, quality services could be provided, and taxpayers could benefit. Giuliani, *"...abandoned New York's failed policies and infused new values, making government work for the benefit of the public in a city long ruled by narrow interests."* (Privatization Bears Fruit in the Big Apple. www.mackinac.org).

The Pros and Cons of Privatization

Government tends to be a large lumbering, politically motivated and slow moving entity, resistant to change and inflexible. Unionization in the government sector is higher than the private sector, and governments tend to have burdensome work rules. Proponents of privatization of public services, argue that private companies, either non-profit or for-profit, have greater accountability, are technologically more sophisticated, can deliver high quality services, with greater flexibility, more efficiently, and at lower cost.

Reasons for Using the Private Sector

- To obtain special skills or supplement staff for short periods.
- To meet demands beyond current government capacity.
- To reduce costs.
- To improve service quality.
- To provide clients with more choice of providers and levels of service.
- Ideology--less government is better.

(http://www.urban.org/publications/407023.html)

Another concern about privatizing is the delivery of quality social services. Those opposed to privatization, also argued that if profit is the motivation, then service quality or delivery methods may be reduced, or a contractor may only accept the most profitable clients. Privatization contracts tend to be based on unit costs, to deliver specific services, per recipient. For example, if a contractor is paid a fixed fee per client served, then the contractor may reduce services, choose the clients most likely to succeed, or less costly to service. In this way, the contractor can go back to the government agency, when the contract is to be renewed, and say they have fully serviced all the clients that qualified. Government agencies, and the contractor, can protect the needs of the clients, and the public, by writing strong contracts with specific performance and responsibilities criteria, and remediation methods, if the required services fail to meet expectations.

Major Arguments for Opposing Privatization

- Major loss of public employee jobs.
- Relinquishes public responsibility for public funds. Private business has no business allocating public funds or monitoring the use of public funds.
- Threatens fiscal accountability.
- Weakens community ability to assert collective interests; decreases citizen participation in government.
- High potential for fraud, financial conflicts-of-interest, and cost overruns.
- Any resulting cost savings are directed away from taxpayers and towards the contractor.
- Threatens confidentiality of private information.
- Financial conflicts of interest.
- Increases temptation to reduce quality of services and accept the best clients to reduce costs and maximize profit.

(http://www.urban.org/publications/407023.html).

Significant opposition to privatization comes from government union leadership. Organized labor views privatization as a method to weaken the union power base by reducing their employment base. *Privatization is another factor adding to the decline of organized labor.*

A report by the National Commission for Employment Policy (1989) found:

- Contracting out public services has caused shrinkage in the rate of growth of the public sector work force since the mid-1970s.
- Job loss in the government is generally offset by job gains in the private sector--for every 10 jobs lost in that state and local government sector due to privatizations, about eight or nine new jobs were created in the private sector.
- Layoffs of public employees due to privatization are uncommon. Affected workers usually take jobs with contractors or transition to jobs in other public agencies, usually through an agreement initiated by the government. Moving to the private sector generally means a reduction in employee benefits, but a modest increase in wages. (http://www.urban.org/publications/407023.html).

"Business does some things better than government, but government does some things better than business. The public sector tends to be better at... policy management, preventing discrimination...ensuring continuity of services, and social cohesion. Business tends to be better at performing economic tasks, innovating, adapting to change, and performing complex or technical tasks. The non-profit sector tends to be best at...tasks that generate little or no profit, and demand compassion,... require extensive trust, and involve the enforcement of moral codes and individual responsibility for behavior." (Osborne and Gaebler 1992). (http://www.urban.org/publications/407023.html).

IS ORGANIZED LABOR A DECAYING BUSINESS MODEL?

Modern government needs to operate with the private sector business model mindset. No longer can local, state, or federal government programs throw money at social problems without significant accountability. Governments on all levels must deal with the economic realities of providing more social services with fewer resources. Government agencies and private companies, offer their own strengths and weaknesses. For privatization to be successful, government agencies must choose the provider based on abilities, accountability, performance, and cost factors. The bottom line for taxpayers and the clients served is to deliver better quality public services for lower costs.

CHAPTER 6

Organize to Survive

Organize or Perish

The future growth business model is to organizing the unorganized, or organize the under organized, in industries and markets that have not been fully utilized, or where the union saturation levels are under utilized. Unions, as with any business, must expand and look for new business and new territories to grow and prosper. For labor unions, it is new members. For retail and service businesses, it is new customers, clients, or accounts.

<u>Organized labor must organize to survive</u>. Organizing is the business model and vehicle for the labor movement to survive and grow. To increase membership, unions must organize more new workers than workers they loose. Union membership is falling rapidly, because of plant closing, union membership buyouts, corporate consolidations, bankruptcy, outsourcing, downsizing, automation, technology, and globalization.

<u>Organized labor is big business</u>. Unions earn money from investments and holdings, but the initial income is earned from dues paying members. Managing a large labor union is similar to running a large diversified company with thousands, or tens of

thousands of stakeholders. Organized labor as a group is a $10 billion per year industry. Labor unions business model is to increase the income, improve the working conditions, and support the needs of its dues paying members. The larger the membership base, the greater the income earned from members dues, and therefore more money to invest in organizing and internal business operation. The larger the membership base, the greater political strength, and the greater social and economic strength. This strength translates to greater bargaining power negotiating contracts with management that benefit the workers whom they serve. The stronger unions have the ability to provide excellent customer service for their members. The better reputation a union has, the more non-union workers seek out a specific union to represent them. Members pay union dues to labor unions because labor unions provide a service to their represented members. That is the reason for their existence.

Organizing is not easy, is extremely expensive, labor intensive, and requires strong commitment from workers wishing to become unionized. At best, it is an uphill fight, requiring professional talent to lead and direct the un-organized to become the newly organized. Corporations fight unionization with professional labor consultants, or *"union busters"* in the union vernacular, to persuade the employees to remain non-union.

Counter Union Organizing Methods

Company management in a non-union company, when confronted with a union organizing drive by their employees, is protecting their desire to remain non-union. Corporations have a few viable options fighting a union organizing drive. They can try to convince employees not to join the union, using in house attorneys, supervisory or management staff. This approach is not very successful, because in house staff is usually unfamiliar with the legal and technical complexities of fighting an organizing drive. In addition, employees over time may have built up a dislike for certain management or supervisors that can create negative feelings towards the company in the minds and hearts of the workers. The negative corporate feelings make it easier for the union to win the organizing campaign. Unions win when company employee relations fail.

Another corporate option is to accept the union, through the *"card check"* method. The company agrees that a majority of the workers wish to be unionized, and company officials amicably negotiate a contract in hopes of a smooth relationship. The rationale is that if labor and management can remain friendly adversaries, perhaps the third party union intervention will be within the financial abilities of the company, and the conditions will be acceptable. This method is the least disruptive and contentious.

The corporate option that offers the greatest success rate to frustrate a union organizing drive, and for the company to remain non-union, is to hire a labor consultant, or in the labor vernacular, a *"union buster."* This is the most disruptive, contentious and expensive method. However, management may view a labor consultant as long-term anti-union insurance. There is also the corporate ego issue to deal with. The management mentality might be something to the effect of, *"It is my company. I built this company, and I will NOT have some third party (the union) telling me how to run things. If the workers do not want to work here, they can quit!"*

On the other side of the spectrum, are the employees who have come to the collective realization that work place issues have come to the point that the only way to solve the problems *is* by joining a union, and engaging in collective representation. The psychological war begins before the union drive begins. An organizing drive can be an emotional experience in which co-workers and friends become polarized. The job of the labor consultant, using the company supervisors and management, is to convince the employees to vote UNION NO. The union organizers job is to convince the employees to vote UNION YES. The union versus management war begins.

The Roles of Labor Relations Consultants or Union Busters

Martin Levitt, author of <u>Confessions of a Union Buster</u> was a professional, well paid labor consultant or *'union buster,'* who exposed the inside strategies used by the consultants. The book provided pro-union employees and union organizers with an educational tool and road map of what to expect when confronted with a professional labor consultant orchestrating the corporate response to a union organizing drive.

Levitt notes that a labor consultant must *"Challenge everything ... take every challenge to a full hearing, then prolong each hearing, and appeal every unfavorable ruling."* (http://www.pww.org/article/articleprint/4255). The idea is to wear down the union and the workers, and make them feel that it is hopeless to organize. Levitt writes, *"Union busting is a field populated by bullies and built on deceit. The only way to bust a union is to lie, distort, manipulate, threaten, and attack. The law does not hamper, but defines strategies. The attacks are personal, they invade peoples live, crush their will, and shatter families."* (http://workers.labor.net.au/67/d_review_costa.html). The labor consulting business is about control. Robert Muehlenkamp, local 1199 union organizer noted, *"You have to appreciate that most people at a worksite are just ordinary people. They have no experience with violence...with being lied to...with being harassed...and insulted...in public."* (http://www.pww.org/article/articleprint/4255).

Union avoidance campaigns are big business. Most corporate managers are unsure how to handle a union problem when confronted with a union organizing drive. Corporate America fails to realize, when there is a union organizing drive the company may not have a union problem, as much as it may have an employee relations problem. That is poor employee relationships with management and supervisors have caused the employees to seek protection from a union. Repressive companies cause strong union relationships with the employees. Good companies, who appreciate their workers, and pay decent salaries consistent with comparable wages in the industry, usually remain union free. Unionization is reduced when companies treated their workers well.

Labor consultant firms offer different methods of selling their services as unique and specialized, and each firm advocates specific techniques for employers to remain non-union, fight an organizing campaign, or decertify an existing union in the company.

"*Proactive and preventative policies are the more constructive way management can avoid a union insurgence,*" advises Sheppard, Mullin, Richter, and Hampton, a labor relations consulting firm. The firm advises clients that, "*Our attorneys have developed a solid reputation for an aggressive, practical, and tactically sound approach to organizing drives and labor disputes in a broad variety of industries... We have been extremely successful in keeping many organizations union free through positive and ongoing management training programs.*" (http://www.smrh.com/practices-105.html).

The Burke Group, established in 1982, claims to be the largest full service labor-consulting firm. They teach companies how to stay union free, or return to union free by winning decertification elections at previously unionized companies. The Burke Group claims a success rate of "*96%, including petition withdrawals, are involved in over 800 U.S. and International union campaigns, with 1300 clients, in 50 industries, and in 10 countries, with over 70 union elections avoided, and 60 successful union decertification elections, and offers a diverse team of bi-lingual consultants.*" (www.tbglabor.com). The Burke Group further advises employers that a happy workforce does not want a union. The best way to achieve this is to "*...treat employees with respect, and to *encourage employee participation in decisions that impact their lives, and compensate employees according to the marketplace, resolve workplace issues, and reward individual performance"* (www.tbglabor.com).

Power Through Information (PTI) specializes in anti-union research, and use PowerPoint presentations that highlight the company's message. The company has developed campaign specific websites that emphasize the benefits of remaining union free. Their websites have remote usage tracking abilities, allowing management to know which employees have logged on. PTI provides customized e-mail, giving employees access to company news, and data the company wishes to use that supports their position. *"Our websites are custom designed to reflect the business vocation, workforce culture, and ethnic diversity"* (http://www.ptilaborresearch.com/research_custom.html). PTI develops customized videos, which reflect the ethnic and cultural diversity of the workers, and claim that 95% of their clients, who use the videos, remain union free. *"One of the most powerful strategic tools in your counter union campaign is a PTI customized labor video... proven to be one of the most effective methods of communicating with your employees."* (http://www.ptilaborresearch.com/home.html).

The goal of organized labor is to organize the employer and <u>not</u> the employee. Unions prefer a *card check* organizing method and neutrality agreement, in lieu of a secret ballot NLRB election. It is faster method, less contentious, less expensive, and labor unions win about 70% of *card check* elections. In a <u>card check</u>, the employer agrees to accept the union as the bargaining agent, and in a <u>neutrality agreement</u>, the employer agrees to maintain a neutral position about the union, and not interfere in the organizing.

Another tactic used by labor consultants during a union organizing campaign is to hire third party *persuaders*. The <u>persuaders</u> communicate directly with employees, in the same manner union organizers talk with employees. Labor relations consultants deal strictly with management, while *persuaders* deal with the employees, and must file with the Labor Department as union organizers. The *persuaders* have similar profiles as the employees, in terms of gender, language, and ethnic background, and speak in the same vernacular as the employees. Because of the affinity relationship, the *persuaders* are excellent at influencing the fence sitters and convincing employees to vote for the union.

The labor consulting business is very profitable. For example, Jackson Lewis, founded in 1958, has 30 offices nationwide, employs over 430 lawyers, and has annual revenues of over $40 million (http://jacksonlewis.com/aboutus/firmfacts.cfm). The firm advocates the tactical advantage of delay. The longer an employer can delay the election, the more time the employer and the labor consultant has to convince the employees that voting against the union is in the employees and companies best interests. Delay takes the fire out of the union organizing campaign, wears down the union activists, and creates an air of hopelessness and confusion amongst employees. Management uses this time to convince employees that they are now listening and care about the workers. (http://www.jacksonlewis.com).

The objective of the labor consultant is to create fear and doubt in the minds of the workers. They create fear that the employees will loose everything they worked so hard to gain. The consultant, using the supervisors and managers as spokespersons, may suggest that because of the added cost of unions, the company may be forced to reduce overtime, cut production, and outsource work. This may affect the workers job security, and salary or benefits. They create doubt in the employees mind, imply that the union will loose the campaign, and give the idea that the company will listen to the employees concerns now that the company is aware of the issues. The corporate position is the union is not necessary because the company wants to take care of their employees, and a third party union would only interfere with the

IS ORGANIZED LABOR A DECAYING BUSINESS MODEL?

new paternal company outlook.

A Workplace Scenario

Labor consultants take full advantage that employees lack knowledge about unions and the law, and play on emotions and friendships with co-workers, company loyalty, economic fear, and job security. The labor consultant may use similar tactics as noted in the following hypothetical scenario. Employees may expect possible captive audience situation such as; "We are a small company. We just invested in a new machine so we can we can make bigger widgets faster. We cannot afford the extra costs that a union will bring. If you vote for the union, we may have to close a division, move the work to Mexico, cut hours, or reduce the work force. Think of how that will affect your standard of living." Management gets personal by saying, "Gee, Bill you just bought a new pick-up last month, and John, you just closed on the brand new four bedroom house in the east end of town, and Mary's daughter needs surgery, and Amy is retiring in a few years. Think about this, how is the union going to help you pay your bills?"

The other tactics employees may encounter can also include various doses of love, hugs, tears, and management begging for forgiveness for the evils of their past ways, as noted in the following imaginary scenario example; "We value our loyal employees and had no idea that you all felt this way. You folks are the backbone of this company. We cannot run American Widgets without your dedicated services. We have been so busy building the business to help our wonderful employees have a better life, that we lost track of certain things." Management gets personal again by saying, "We take care of our employees. Why just last month we gave John his promotion to line leader, so he could buy that nice new four-bedroom house on the east end of town. Bill received a wage increase and bought that shiny new red Ford pick-up truck." The company shows credibility, especially with the selected employees who are respected by their fellow workers.

The hard sell begins. "Gee, would a union be able to do all that for our loyal employees? I do not think so! Bill, John, Mary and Amy, what do you think? Would a union be able to do all that for you? NO! American Widgets really cares about our employees. In fact, a new employee committee has just been formed called Team American Widgets, which will help management make the needed improvements you all want. You really do not need a union telling you what to do. We take care of our own."

"All the union wants is your hard-earned money for dues, so some fat cat in the big city can drive his new Cadillac and buy his mistress a new fur coat. The variations to this theme are to use the ethnic, gender or race card. This is a very powerful motivating factor, especially if the employees are primarily of a specific minority, gender, or ethnic background, or if a specific minority, gender, or ethnic entity manages or owns the company. The labor consultant will have the supervisors show the union is white, or male, or for or against a specific group, and will use whatever hook is needed to create a racial, ethnic, social or gender divide. The job of the labor consultant is to *Divide and Conquer* by creating confusion or doubt in the minds of the workers. This technique is very effective.

One-on-One Meetings

One-on-one meetings involve a supervisor and employee, and therefore it is very difficult to prove what was actually said or promised. A theoretical case in point may consist of supervisor, Mr. Jones talking with employee Mary and saying; "...Mary, I would like to know what you are really thinking and feeling. This is just a friendly little chat and nothing we talk about will ever leave this room. Mary, you have worked here at American Widgets for fifteen years, and your employment record is excellent. That is why I would like to chat with you. Tell me, what do you think of all

IS ORGANIZED LABOR A DECAYING BUSINESS MODEL?

this union stuff? Do you think we really need a union at American Widgets? What will a union do except take your money? Have you really looked at that union organizer? What's up with that ugly scar on his neck?" It does not matter if the union organizer is a veteran and that scar is a combat wound. The objective is to discredit the union by whatever means necessary.

The one-on-one meeting may continue, with the supervisor saying, "Mary, remember two years ago, when your daughter broke her arm on the school play ground and had to be rushed to the hospital? Do you remember that your insurance would not cover the physical therapy she needed after surgery and how I went around to all your co-workers and took up a collection to help you out? Do you also remember that you did not have any sick leave left and American Widgets donated sick time so you could be with your daughter? Do you really think that guy from the union would do that for you? I don't think so! We take care of our own, and we are family. Only you're friends at American Widgets care about you, and not some union guy from the big city. All the union guy wants is your money for dues, so he can get rich. Do you know that the union dues will be $100 per month taken out of your paycheck? That is a lot of money. What will you get for your dues money? He does not even know you, so how can he care about you or your friends here."

Mary may respond by thanking Mr. Jones and the good folks at *American Widgets* for their kindness. Mary may say; "I am not sure about the union. We do need someone listening to our needs on the shop floor. Maybe the union might help. That new super widget machine is just too fast and my arms hurt at the end of the day. I told Bob, the line supervisor, and he yelled at me and said I should stop whining and just do my job, or he would transfer me back to the night shift. So I said, 'Yes Sir' and went back to work. I would be happy, if we could slow that machine down a bit."

Mr. Jones responds, "I will talk with Bob. He should not yell at you and I will make sure you do not work the night shift. See, we *really do care about our people at American Widgets. I am sure glad you came to me and we had this little talk. See how easy it is to solve your problems by just talking with me. I bet this will never happen if a third party outsider union takes control of American Widgets. Do you agree? Mary, can I count on your voting union no, and joining the Team American Widgets committee that can solve all your problems? Please tell your friends, and have a great afternoon."*

At this point, Mr. Jones has successfully guilt tripped Mary and she may start to accept Mr. Jones reasoning. This is the objective. Mary will go back to her co-workers and re-tell the story, feeling proud of how *American Widgets* and Mr. Jones care about the workers needs, and how joining *Team American Widgets* committee might solve all the problems. Mr. Jones can report to the labor consultant that he just convinced Mary to vote union "no," and she will probably convince her friends.

Do these scenarios sound far fetched? *Think again!* The basis of the consultants work is to convince the employees that unions are evil and the company is good. It is very real and very believable especially to employees who have not heard these tactics before. It is human nature to forgive and give one more chance. The employees may reason that management at *American Widgets* must care about the workers.

Guess what probably will happen if the workers vote NO for the union? The people, whom management and the consultant tagged as pro-union, eventually, are not working for *American Widgets*, as the company replaces them with non-union workers. Over time, the pro-union workers will be defused, and things will return to business as usual, perhaps with small changes made.

A union organizing attempt is a wake up call to management they need to change their employee relations procedures. If the union loses, the company returns to the way it was. To avoid future unionization attempts, management may have to show they care about their employees. If the union wins, the labor consultant will advise managers to delay a first contract, or decertify the union, in hopes of wearing down the union.

First Contracts and Decertifying a Union

Labor consultants are hired by a company to persuade employees <u>not</u> to join a union. In this regard, labor consultants have numerous persuasion methods, mostly legal, or if not legal, are without significant consequences for the company or the consultant. Labor consultants have a very high win rate, depending on the consulting firm chosen, and the resolve and resources of the employer.

If a union already exists in a company, the consultants' job is to prevent the signing of a first contract, or convince workers they must decertify the existing union. The true union strength is in the contract, and the first contract sets the groundwork for future contracts, and is therefore very important. If the union wins the campaign and NLRB certified as a bargaining agent, but there is no first contract, then there are no established work rules, salaries or other collective bargaining features. Essentially the union is in place, without any basis or methods of control. It is a union in name only, with no power, no authority, and will soon become irrelevant. The labor consultant is very aware of this, and advises the company to stall on first contract negotiation. The object is to wear out the union and demoralize the union supporters, so eventually they give up.

During this process, the company is also looking for ways to intimidate, terminate, transfer, change shift schedules or assignments, and other methods to reduce the effectiveness of the ardent pro-union employees. The military tactic of *Divide and Conquer* applies. The company separates the pro-union employees from the regular workers, and pairs the regular workers with the pro-company employees. This seemingly harmless schedule changes works to convince the regular workers to support the company and not the union.

The other tactic used by labor consultants is to have a union _decertified_, or dissolved as the bargaining agent representing company employees. The National Labor Relations Board (NLRB) specifies the methods and rules for decertifying an existing union from the workplace. "The filing of a petition seeking... decertification of a union should be accompanied by a sufficient showing of interest to support such a petition. Support is typically demonstrated by submitting dated signatures of at least 30% of employees in the bargaining unit in favor of... decertify a currently recognized union." (http://www.nlrb.gov/Workplace_Rights/i_am_new_to_this_website/how_do_i_file_a_petition_to_start_or_remove_a_union.aspx).

Through the process of _Divide and Conquer_, the company eventually gets the pro-company (anti-union) employees to seek an NLRB petition for decertification. This procedure works well if the union resolve is weaker, and the company resources are stronger, or if there has been little or no progress obtaining a meaningful first contract. The company, through peer pressure, intimidation, attrition, transfer, termination, or other methods, reduces the strength of the pro-union workers, and increases the support of the anti-union workers. Newly hired workers are screened for their union empathy. The only workers left are those who are convinced that the union is evil and the company is good.

However, if the union is strong and aggressively supports the employees, or if the company is weak or inept, and continuously appears to the workers as an evil entity, then union decertification becomes difficult. Corporate behavior determines the strength of the union. There is an axiom that says, _repressive management welcomes strong unions, and good management does not welcome unions_. The bottom line is employees seek unions as protection from repressive management decisions and poor labor relations practices.

Love Tactics and Scare Tactics

Labor consultants techniques generally follow a time line script, and include variations of *love tactics and scare tactics*, intended to influence the employees to VOTE UNION NO. The *love tactics* may include pleas by the employer to give them another chance. The employer admits to their past mistakes, saying they have been too busy building the company, and they have neglected their most important asset-their loyal employees. They promise to correct their past mistakes, and it will never happen again, if only the employees would be so nice as to forgive the company and vote union no. Since the company is changing their attitudes towards the employees, and things are improving, perhaps management is correct, and the workers may reason they do not need the union. Ask an attorney how effective creating *reasonable doubt* is in the courtroom. Creating doubt is a very effective method to *Divide and Conquer* the workplace (http://www.ufcw.org/get_a_union/organizing_101/typical_campaign/index.cfm).

The opposite side of the same coin is *scare tactics*. Management might say that even if the employees are successful in bring a union to the company, management does not have to bargain with the union, may not comply with any contract, and the union will have little power. The company states that the accountants recommend to stay in business the company may have to outsource work, hire temporary workers, eliminate overtime, or reduce hours. The object is to scare the workers with job loss, or income loss. Of course, what management does not tell the workers is that federal law requires the company to abide by a union contract and the company cannot threaten job loss if the union wins.

The labor consultant works behind the scenes, and uses company management and supervisors as the spokesperson. The consultant places a heavy responsibility on the front line supervisors, who must convince their subordinates that unions are evil, and the supervisor's job and future depend on the employer remaining union free. Management *scare tactics* may include information about excessive dues, union criminal activities, or unions create strikes and workers loose money during a strike. Management proclaims now that it is aware of how employees feel, things will be much better in the future. The underlying message is that things would be happier if the union was not trying to disrupt the workplace. Workers get tired of the tension and want peace and a return to some form of normalcy. *Love tactics* and *scare tactics* techniques are very effective anti-union tools.

Expected Time Line of Events

<u>The last four weeks</u> are the most critical in a union organizing campaign. Every campaign is unique, but there is a definite game plan and time line of events. The NLRB has determined the eligible employees, and an election date, time and location has been set. *"Within seven days after an election has been ordered, the employers must submit a list of names and addresses of all employees in the bargaining unit to the National Labor Relations Board regional director. This list is known as the <u>"Excelsior List"</u>...named after the 'Excelsior Underwear Company' (1966) and...provides a basis for resolving disputes about the eligibility of employees ...before the election"* (A Training Manual for Union Organizers, p. 84).

The consultant rarely show their face on the shop floor, therefore the role of the supervisor is one of the main anti-union ingredients used by management to win a union campaign. *"Management consultants rely on the company supervisors to be the eyes, ears and mouthpiece in their efforts to defeat a union organizing campaign...they have direct, daily contact with the employee. They provide management with detailed reports on the behavior and attitude of each employee...and this information is used to plan the next stages of the campaign"* (A Training Manual for Union Organizers, pp. 71-72).

<u>The last three weeks</u> of the campaign get more intense. Union

supporters by this time have been fired, or their shift and work locations changed to restrict their contact with the other workers. The *Divide and Conquer* technique is a very effective deterrent and a psychological message to the workers of what life may be like if the union wins. Organizing campaigns are based on winning the hearts and minds of the workers.

Captive audience and one-on-one meetings continue and management will stress the evils of unions and the bad effects a unionized workforce will have on their business. The company will imply that because of the added costs, they may have to reduce production based on economic conditions, meaning they may have to reduce shifts, move production to another country, or in some way, cause jobs to be lost. This creates fear of the unknown in the workers minds, and creates fear that they may loose their job if the union wins the election. The message is that it is better to deal with the devil known, than the devil unknown. Fear is a very powerful motivator, and labor consultants understand the psychological impact of fear, and use it to their advantage.

The labor consultant will usually advise management to form a <u>*Vote Union No Committee*</u> to create further employee polarization and unrest. *"Under the law, the anti-union group can act virtually in the same manner as the union; it can circulate petitions, and anti-union literature, urge employees to vote union no, and qualify for a place on the ballot"* (A Training Manual for Union Organizers, p. 73). The union can counter act this by having workers wear *Union Yes* T-shirts, buttons and caps to show unyielding union solidarity (http://www.corporatecampaign.org/bust3.htm).

To soften the perceived economic advantage of higher wages and better benefits offered in union companies, consultants often advise management to raise wages and benefits on par with a union shop in the same industry or nearby location. Happy workers do not need a union, is the message. This method proves to employees that a union is unnecessary because management has taken this action without the need of a union, and "*employees who feel that their pay and benefits programs are inadequate are prime prospects for union organizers*" (A Training Manual for Union Organizers, p. 72).

The employer is exploiting the one-on-one conversations, in which a supervisor engages in a sincere talk with employees privately. "*Experience has shown that one of the best ways a company has to indoctrinate its employees against the union is by having every supervisor engage in heart-to-heart talks with each employee under his charge*" (A Training Manual for Union Organizers, p. 73). This method is extremely effective when used in conjunction with the captive audience meetings. The objective is for management to listen to individual employee complaints, and to show genuine concern and respect for the individual employee. Of course, this gives management an accurate consensus of which employee or groups of employees are pro union, anti union or undecided.

<u>During the second week</u>, the war for the hearts and minds of the workers becomes more intense. Management will circulate horror stories of bad unions, or companies that went broke after the union won the election or some other version that casts a negative image of the particular union that is organizing at the workplace. This is a continuation of the message that unions are evil, greedy, corrupt, and bad for the workers. The union organizers can counter act this message, by providing "*...believable testimonies of real people who speak from their own experience about union pride and achievements*" (http://www.corporatecampaign.org/bust4.htm).

An effective method used by the consultants is the <u>payday surprise</u>. In this scenario, the employer hands out the paychecks and someone shout out they have been shortchanged in their pay envelope. The boss, then hands out a second envelope, which is the amount of money the union would take out for dues. The concept is to allow the employees to visualize the amount of money they would have to pay in union dues and fees if they vote union yes. The employer points out that the employees will loose this amount every paycheck. The consultants call this tactic *"the split paycheck stuffer"* (http://www.corporatecampaign.org/bust4.htm).

<u>One week before the election</u>, expect the unexpected. The final week is a no holds barred contest by the company for employee loyalty and a union no vote. During this time, the tensions are high which can further provoke anti union violence, aggressive behavior, verbal abuse, sexual harassments, and employee polarization. The union must promote non-violence and advocate solidarity. Fear of violence is a strong form of psychological intimidation and the union must advocate peaceful coexistence.

With less than a week before the election, both the union and management are aggressively campaigning for the group of employees identified as undecided. At this time, the union should be doing intense home visits, and reaching out for community support. Both sides are looking to push hot button issues. This is an intense political contest for employee votes. The employer will increase the pressure and ask for forgiveness, noting that the process has opened their eyes and increased their awareness of the issues, and promise to listen to the workers needs, if only they would just give the company a chance and vote union no.

Usually a few days before the election, the company will send out its top official, such as the unseen owner, or CEO. This person will proclaim *"Because of the sensitive legal issues, the company is prohibited from making any promises, but please understand that your concerns have not gone unnoticed, and if you please support the company now, great changes will happen in the future"* (http://www.corporatecampaign.org/bust5.htm).

The union organizers must do everything possible to convince employees to vote union yes during the last week of the drive. The labor consultant must do everything possible to convince employees to vote against the union. The union must convince the undecided that the union is the best way to protect workers rights.

The labor consultant must convince the undecided workers that the union is a bad choice for the workers and for the company, and the only viable option is to vote union no. The outcome of the election must be certain before the election. The ballot box is the not the time to convince the swing voters. (http://www.corporate-campaign.org/bust5.htm).

Myths and Facts about Unions

The labor consultant is directing supervisors and management in the anti-union campaign, and is questioning employees about why they need a union at the company. Union organizers need to be prepared with answers. The AFL-CIO publication, Myths and Facts about Unions, is a useful tool for union organizers and union advocates.

For example, the company will paint the union as an outsider, or special interest group. The union response is that the workers collectively are the union. The company may say unions create conflict in the workplace. The union response is that unions can make the workplace run smoother, because the contract regulates the working conditions and this reduces conflict. The company may state that unions force workers to strike. Unions' response is that workers determine a strike, not the union, and 97% of contract disputes are settled without a strike. Strikes are the avenue of last resort. The company may say that unions cause companies to close. The unions response is that companies close because of poor management and for economic reasons and a majority that close are non-union.

According to Cornell University scholar Kate Bronfenrenner, only 1% of newly organized plants close. The company will say that unions only want your money. The union response is that unions are not-for-profit organizations and dues pay the operational expenses. Union workers usually enjoy increases in pay, benefits, and job security. Average union workers make about 25% more than non-union workers, women and African American workers earn about 30% more, and Latino workers earn about 45% more than non-union workers. Currently, about 12% of the total workforce is unionized. (www.aflcio.org/aboutunion.cfm).

After the Vote

If the union loses the election, the likely scenario will be the union supporters will be laid-off, terminated, or transferred to another location or shift. The company will return to business as usual. Organizing campaigns are often corporate wake up calls, and a progressive company may learn from the experience and choose to listen to the needs of the employees, in hopes of avoiding another conflict. Things may change for the better, such as improved wages or working conditions, and the company may establish new employee procedures. Less progressive companies, may choose to fire all the pro-union workers for various reasons, and return to the repressive company they were before the union organizing campaign. New employee policies may include screening newly hired workers for their union feelings, and hiring only workers who express a strong anti-union sentiment. In this way, they hope to avoid future organizing attempts.

A method often used by companies to make the lay-offs or terminations not look too obvious, and thus avoid legal problems, will be to reduce production for a period, and cut shifts or work hours. Less production translates to fewer workers needed, and the terminations or reduced hours can be legally justified. This is a viable method for the employer to reduce the workforce as needed, remove the union supporters, and less productive or more expensive workers. It also sends a clear message to the remaining employees that this employer will not tolerate unionization attempts.

If the union wins the election, the company has a few choices. The employer can express disappointment in the outcome, reduce production, or outsource functions. This will result in staff reductions, via lay-offs or terminations, with the vague promise to rehire those employees once business improves. As part of the production cuts, the union supporters will usually be laid-off or terminated, as will a few of the less productive or more expensive workers. This spreads the lay-offs over a wider group, and may avoid the obvious fact that the union supporters are being fired.

A progressive company may choose to recognize defeat and accept the labor union as the bargaining agent for the employees. In this manner, it is felt, that negative feelings developed during the organizing drive, can be put behind them. The company may reason, moving forward, it is better to develop a positive relationship, which in the final analysis, benefits all the players. A harmonious working relationship may help win a favorable First Contract, which the employer and employees can accept.

The NLRB has ruled the firing of union supporters as an *Unfair Labor Practice* (ULP) and therefore illegal. After lengthy NLRB legal action, the usual remedy is to award the illegally terminated employee back pay, and/or returned to their previous position. The legal concept is known as making the employee *whole*. When an employee is *made whole*, it usually means the employee receives back pay equal to the same rate of pay they had prior to being terminated, up to the time of settlement. For example, if the employee earned a salary of $50,000 per year and the settlement took two years, then the employee would be awarded $100,000, the amount equal to the salary they had earned prior to the illegal termination of the employee. The back pay is less any income the former employee earned prior to settlement from other employment or unemployment insurance. In this example, if the employee had earned $40,000 from other employment and/or unemployment insurance, then the final settlement would be $60,000. If the employee is returned to work, they must be offered the same rate of pay and level of benefits to which they would have been entitled to had their employment been uninterrupted, including a schedule consisting of approximately the same number of hours they previously worked. The employee is legally *made whole* in this example.

The company may choose to fight a *first contract*. A *first contract* is important, in that it sets the precedence for future labor agreements with the employer. If there is no *first contract*, then in realty there are no established work rules, wage scales, or collective bargaining relationships. The newly elected union is a union in name only, with no power or authority with the employer. Over time, the employer can still operate as usual, and put pressure on employees. The company goals are to frustrate the negotiation process, and therefore dampen the resolve of the union and the union supporters. Labor consultants strongly advise employers to fight a *first contract*. The employer often hires the same labor firm that orchestrated the failed union organizing drive, to represent the company in the *first contract* negotiations. The labor consultant, after losing the election, bills the company to stall the negotiations and delay a *first contract*. Stalling tactics may include agreeing to minor items, but holding fast on the important issues, or simply refusing to negotiate in a timely manner. Win or loose the organizing drive, the consultants are again paid for their services to delay a *first contract*. Without a first contract, the union over time fads away and the company wins. The company goes back to business as usual.

Weingarten Rights

Section 7 of the National Labor Relations Act (NLRA), legally grants a union employee protection when confronted with management over a disciplinary issue that may result in an adverse action taken against the unionized employee. The Supreme Court in 1975 in a landmark employee rights case, NLRB v. J Weingarten, Inc., held that union employees have the right to union representation in meetings with management that may result in a disciplinary action against the employee. The case is known as _Weingarten Rights_. The employee has the exclusive legal right, and management cannot determine the necessity or deny the employee the ability to exercise this right. The law states, "*If any discussion with a supervisor could in any way lead to my being disciplined or terminated, or affect my personal working conditions, I request that my union representative, officer or shop steward be present at this meeting. Without representation present, I choose not to participate in this discussion.*" (NLRB v. Weingarten). The Weingarten Rights remains an important and effective employee protection law.

The Weingarten Rights does not apply to public sector employees employed by state governments, because similar separate state laws may be in effect protecting those union employees. (http://www.jacksonlewis.com/legalupdates/article.cfm?aid=1075). The NLRB has determined that non-union employees do not have legal protection under _Weingarten Rights_. The law only grants unionized employees the right to have union representation in a meeting with management that in the employees view may result in adverse action. (http://www.lawfirmalliance.com/assets/attachments/81.pdf).

To summarize, union wages are generally higher than non-union wages, which has helped create the American middle class. Corporate America is always searching for less expensive business methods, to reduce production costs and labor costs, and thus increase profits. Globalization, outsourcing, downsizing, privatization, and technology are some of the various challenges facing organized labor. These challenges have contributed to the decline of organized labor, because unionized workers are unable to compete competitively with workers in low-wage nations or low-wage states.

On the other side, companies will spend vast resources to remain non-union. The labor consulting business is big business. Non-union employers have greater flexibility to meet changing business cycles, and can take advantage of outsourcing and globalization. Non-union employers create jobs, but may not create significant middle class wealth in the community, because wages and benefits are usually lower than unionized employers are.

The bottom line is that organizing is the labor union business model to increase union membership. One must remember that organized labor is big business. *Organize or Perish* is the mantra for growth and success. Organizing new union members is the corporate equivalent to seeking new business or new clients. Union members are labor unions business and their clients. Strong labor unions are able to implement strong labor contracts. The greater the membership, the larger the political power and economic base needed to win elections and support labor centric candidates and issues.

CHAPTER 7

Politics and Labor Unions

Unions and Political Money

Organized labor is a major political supporter. Labor unions collectively contribute vast sums of financial, human resources, and in-kind services, for political support on the national, state, and local levels. It is very common for labor unions to staff phone banks, organize mass mailings, support voter turnout drives, and go door to door to support a political candidate, a party, or specific union centric issue. *"...If you apply cost accounting to what the unions do in a political way ... you will find that the non cash contributions consist of staff time, meaning union officials assigned to campaigns for months, printing costs, postage, telephone and various support services financed entirely with union dues and fees."* (http://www.nrtw.org/d/political_spending.htm).

Labor unions contribute 5 % to 50%, with the average of 15%, of membership dues on political support. *"Organized labor income runs about $10 billion a year. Five percent of that is $500 million in dues dollars on politics each election cycle."* (http://www.unionfreeamerica.com/duesforpolitics.htm). Rutgers University professor of economics, Leo Troy made this $500 million estimate in 1996. *"The National Institute for Labor Relations Research estimated that total union political expenditures reached $925 million in the 2004 cycle ... According to The Center for Responsive Politics, eight of the top ten all-time political contributors are labor unions."* (http://www.unionfacts.com/articles/unionPolitics.cfm).

Union PAC Contributions to Federal Candidates 2003-2004 Election Cycle

Number of Political Action Committees (PAC) Making Contributions: 186

Building Trade Unions	$4,907,274	81% (to Dem)	19% (to Rep)
Industrial Unions	$4,306,180	97% (to Dem)	3% (to Rep)
Transportation Unions	$6,208,727	77% (to Dem)	22% (to Rep)
Public Sector Unions	$4,118,526	80% (to Dem)	20% (to Rep)
Other Unions	$1,861,800	88% (to Dem)	12% (to Rep)
Total to Democrats:	**$17,875,259**	**84%**	
Total to Republicans:	**$3,474,898**	**16%**	
Total Amount:	**$21,402,507**		

(Based on data released by the Federal Election Commission on Monday, March 29, 2004)
(http://www.opensecrets.org/industries/indus.asp?Ind=P)

To put union political spending in perspective, the AFL-CIO, in the last <u>four days</u> leading up to the 2006 elections contributed, *"...more than 187,000 union volunteers, who made 7.9 million phone calls, knocked on 3.5 million doors, and reached 2 million workers. The bottom line was an energized and mobilized union vote that made a difference in almost every close race in 2006. One in four voters nationwide was a union member, even though unions make up only 12 % of the workforce, and three-quarters of them voted Democratic. The AFL-CIO and SEIU together spent about $100 million."* (http://www.tompaine.com/articles/2007/01/22/muzzling_unions.php).

Election Cycle Spending from 1990 to 2006

In the 1990 election cycle, total contributions were $41,413,457, with $124,222 from individual donations, and $41,289,235 from PACs, and no soft money donations. Donations to Democrats totaled $38,318,394 and Republicans received $3,034,172. This represents a ratio of 93% for Democrats and 7% of the donations going to Republican federal candidates.

The contributions increased in the 1996 federal election cycle, to a total amount of $64,957,699. Individuals gave only $406,529, with $55,003,484 from PACs, and soft money contributions totaling $9,547,686. The Democrats received $60,600,756 or 94%, and the Republicans received $4,164,680 or 6% of the contributions.

The 2000 election cycle saw total contributions increase to $90,187,531, with individual donations of $744,722, as compared to PAC donations totaling $59,023,914, and soft money contributions adding another $30,418,895. The Democrats enjoyed total donations of $84,900,112 or 94% and the Republican federal candidates received only 6% or $5,073,944.

The 2006 election cycle saw a significant decline in total contributions to $66,302,308, with only $360,287 from individuals, as compared to $65,942.021 from PACs. Democrats received 87% of the donations totaling $57,546,053, compared to the Republicans $8,198,859 or 13%. The Democrats were still favored by organized labor, but the Republican federal candidates have received a slightly higher percentage. This may be attributed to politically stronger Republican candidates, or slightly weaker Democratic candidates, or organized labors desire to hedge their bets between both parties.

The total financial contributions to federal candidates for the election cycles from 1990 to 2006 were huge, amounting to $586,258,242. Individuals gave $4,223,367; contributions from PACs totaled $487,146,356, while soft money contributions were $94,888,519. Total donations to the Democrats were $539,755,533, while Republican donations were $44,220,828, with the Democrats enjoying 92% of the donations, and the Republicans received only 8%. Clearly, labor unions PACs favor the Democrats. (http://www.opensecrets.org/industries/contrib.asp?Ind=P&cycle=2006)

Top 20 Union Contributors PACs in 2006

1.	Intl Brotherhood of Electrical Workers	$3,224,536	97% (Dem)	3% (Rep)
2.	Laborers Union	$2,976,750	86% (Dem)	13% (Rep)
3.	Operating Engineers Union	$2,861,245	79% (Dem)	21% (Rep)
4.	American Federation of Teachers	$2,589,748	99% (Dem)	1% (Rep)
5.	Carpenters & Joiners Union	$2,556,673	74% (Dem)	25% (Rep)
6.	AFSCME	$2,390,338	98% (Dem)	1% (Rep)
7.	National Education Assn	$2,371,427	87% (Dem)	13% (Rep)
8.	United Auto Workers	$2,311,490	99% (Dem)	1% (Rep)
9.	Teamsters Union	$2,276,522	90% (Dem)	10% (Rep)
10.	National Air Traffic Controllers Assn	$2,160,570	76% (Dem)	24% (Rep)
11.	International Assn of Fire Fighters	$2,142,105	72% (Dem)	28% (Rep)
12.	Machinists/Aerospace Workers Union	$2,089,509	98% (Dem)	2% (Rep)
13.	Plumbers/Pipefitters Union	$2,088,170	91% (Dem)	9% (Rep)
14.	Air Line Pilots Assn	$1,819,250	80% (Dem)	20% (Rep)
15.	Sheet Metal Workers Union	$1,771,700	95% (Dem)	5% (Rep)
16.	American Postal Workers Union	$1,749,000	96% (Dem)	4% (Rep)
17.	United Food & Commercial Workers	$1,733,805	98% (Dem)	2% (Rep)
18.	National Assn of Letter Carriers	$1,720,800	88% (Dem)	12% (Rep)
19.	Service Employees International Union	$1,700,392	92% (Dem)	8% (Rep)
20.	Communications Workers of America	$1,678,930	98% (Dem)	2% (Rep)

(http://www.opensecrets.org/industries/contrib.asp?Ind=P&cycle=2006)

The total amount of Political Action Committee (PAC) monies contributed to federal candidates in 2006, by the top 20 unions was $44,212,960. This averaged out to $2,210,648 for each union, with an average of 89.65% donated to the Democratic candidates and 10.35% to Republican candidates. Once again, it is clear that organized labor favors the Democrats.

The underlying point is that organized labor still wields tremendous political and economic strength, and candidates feel they need union endorsements to win elections. The more important and the more contested the race, or issue, the more politicians compete for labor union attention, resources, and support. A political candidate, or union cause, can enlist the services of hundreds of union volunteers, and receive huge financial backing from unions. The organized labor generated political machine is invaluable to candidates or political causes, in terms of monies received and donated volunteer labor. Labor unions have the staffing and financial resources to place hundreds, thousands, or even tens of thousands of foot soldiers on the streets of virtually any city or town in America, knocking on doors, polling, or politicking. As a group, labor unions have the power to get out the vote, and can be very influential in helping a candidate, party or cause win or loose an election. Organized labor needs strong political support to get pro labor legislation passed, and anti-labor initiatives defeated. Politicians need union support to be elected, and unions need political support for legislation. It is a mutually beneficial relationship.

Important Legal Decisions Affecting the Labor Business Model

The Beck Decision

As a condition of employment, the National Labor Relations Act (Section 8 (a) (3)), allows an employer and a union to require all bargaining unit employees pay union dues, even if the employee does not wish to join the union. The employee, who chooses not to become a union member, must pay an <u>agency fee</u> equal to union dues. This is referred to as a <u>union security clause</u>, intended to prevent non-union members from enjoying union benefits, without paying their fair share of the costs. The legal issue was a portion of the <u>agency fee</u> or <u>union dues</u> used for political purposes only, which an employee may not wish to contribute.

In 1988, the Supreme Court affirmed that a dues paying union member could <u>not</u> be forced to pay a portion of their dues, used for political purposes only, when that contradicts with the union members beliefs. *Beck v. Communications Workers of America*, or the Beck decision, became a landmark case for workers rights. The union members *"…alleged that expenditure of their fees on activities such as organizing the employees of other employers, lobbying for labor legislation, social, charitable, and political events violated CWA's duty of fair representation, 8(a)(3), and the First Amendment."* (http://www.campaignfinancesite.org/court/communication1.html).

The Court ruled that political contributions cannot be mandatory and must be voluntarily. The ruling meant *"…unions could not force workers to pay dues to support political causes…unrelated to the normal union duties of collective bargaining and union representation. In Mr. Beck's case, the union spent 79 % of his money for purposes other than normal union duties."* (http://www.cltg.org/cltg/unions/howitaffectsyou.htm).

Another worker who sued was awarded $8,877.43 in back dues, the union used for political contributions. <u>The Beck decision recognized the rights of union workers to pay only dues needed for a union's employee representation duties</u>. *"…fees to support union expenditures unrelated to workplace representation, such as political, social, or charitable contributions, are not mandatory."* (http://www.mackinac.org/article.aspx?ID=1401).

The Beck decision does *not* require unions to notify members of their rights, and therefore the responsibility is up to the individual union member. This has led to wide spread abuse, and several states have enacted _paycheck protect_ measures. These measures help"... *safeguard worker rights by requiring unions to obtain upfront, written approval from individual workers before they spend dues money on political or other non-workplace-related activities.*" (http://www.mackinac.org/article.aspx?ID=1401).

Davenport Decision

The decision involves the Washington Education Association (WEA), a public sector union representing teachers in Washington State. _Agency Fees_ are fees paid in lieu of dues, by represented employees who do not wish to join the union, and are equivalent to the normal union dues paid by union members. Charging an *agency fee* prevents _free riding_, in which a non-union member enjoys the benefits of a unionized work place, without paying their fair share of the costs. The Washington State Fair Campaign Practices Act prohibits public sector unions in that state from using non-union member's money for political purposes, unless given express permission by the non-union member. This procedure, known as _Affirmative Authorization,_ requires the union to inform members they have the right to opt-out and receive a refund, for that portion of their agency fees used for political activities. "*At issue ...was the constitutionality of a unique feature of the Washington state campaign finance law. The state law required public sector unions to obtain the express consent of non-member agency fee payers before spending the non-members' fees in connection with state elections.*" (http://www.aflcio.org/mediacenter/prsptm/pr06142007.cfm).

At issue are the First Amendment rights of unions, _and_ of non-union members who do not wish to support a political activity. Labor unions have First Amendment rights to advocate and support specific political parties or union centric causes. The other side of the coin is the First Amendment rights of non-union members who do not want to be associated with political advocacy.

IS ORGANIZED LABOR A DECAYING BUSINESS MODEL?

A group of non-union member education employees sued for a refund of union fees. "*The Supreme Court* (on June 14, 2007) *reversed* (the previous ruling in 2000), *holding that it does not violate the First Amendment for a State to require that its public-sector unions receive Affirmative Authorization from a non-member before spending that non-member's agency fees for election-related purposes.*" Justice Scalia, who wrote the opinion of the court, further reasoned, "*...the public-sector agency-shop arrangement, authorizing a union to levy fees on government employees who do not wish to join the union, grants an unusual power to a private entity to in essence . . . tax government employees.*" (http://www.scotusblog.com/movabletype/archives/2007/06/more_on_the_dec_2.html). The Supreme Court decision will have little affect any current labor union practices.

Kentucky River Decision

The big picture of the Kentucky River decision has to do with the legal definition of a <u>Supervisor</u>. The case has the potential to prohibit or restrict almost 8 million workers from unionization. A union employee reclassified legally from <u>employee</u> to <u>supervisor</u>, will effectively become non-union, and therefore not represented by a collective bargaining agreement. When a union is trying to organize workers in a company, legally <u>supervisors</u> are not eligible to join and cannot participate in any union organizing activities.

The National Labor Relation Act (NLRA 29 USC 152 (3)), permit *employees* to join unions, but prohibit *supervisors*. (http://www.epinet.org/content.cfm/ib225). Supervisors are considered management, and <u>not</u> employees. The NLRA defines supervisor as: "*...any individual having authority, in the interest of the employer, to hire, transfer, suspend, lay off, recall, promote, discharge, assign, reward, or discipline other employees, or responsibly to direct them, or to adjust their grievances, or effectively to recommend such action, if in connection with the foregoing the exercise*

114

of such authority is not of a merely routine or clerical nature, but requires the use of independent judgment. (29 USC 152 (11))." (Supervisors in Name Only. EPI Briefing Paper #225).

The three separate cases included the Oakland Healthcare Inc, which involved registered nurses acting as *charge nurses* in a hospital. Golden Crest Healthcare Center, which involved Registered Nurses (RN), and Licensed Practical Nurses (LPN), acting as *charge nurses* in a long-term care facility. Croft Metals, Inc. involved workers acting as *lead men* and *load supervisors* in a manufacturing company.

The three cases are collectively referred to as the <u>Kentucky River</u> decision. The National Labor Relations Board ruled in the Oakland Healthcare, Inc., case that nurses legally <u>are</u> *supervisors*, because they often must make *independent judgments* about a patient. An example used was a charge nurse saying, *"Yes, that patient is going into cardiac arrest so I better do something,"* and then telling other nurses or technicians what to do. The NLRB ruled the charge nurse was legally a *supervisor* because they directed others to do something. The same NLRB logic applied to the manufacturing workers at Croft Metals, Inc., because they were directing other workers to do some action like loading trucks or follow instructions. (http://workinglife.typepad.com/daily_blog/2006/10/kentucky_river_.html).

These employees are not really supervisors, except in name only. They do not have management prerogatives, such as the ability to *"...to hire, transfer, suspend, lay off, recall, promote, discharge, assign, reward, or discipline other employees, or responsibly to direct them, or to adjust their grievances, or effectively to recommend such action...,"* as NLRB 29 USC 152 (11), describes a *supervisor*. (Supervisors in Name Only. EPI Briefing Paper #225). The employees on occasion, and as part of their job, use *"independent judgment"* because they *"responsibly direct other employees"* to perform limited functions. (http://www.epinet.org/content.cfm/ib225).

Skilled workers, registered nurses for example, direct other hospital employees, such as orderlies or medical technicians, to perform certain tasks directly related to the care of the patients. The same is true about journeymen construction workers, because they direct and train less skilled trades, as part of doing their daily job routine. These workers are not tasked with making management or supervisory decisions, regarding hiring, or firing, and they have little ability to punish or reward other employees.

The Kentucky River decisions can affect workers in other trades or skills. For example, radio and TV news reporters, or broadcasters, may direct a photographer to shoot a news conference or a house fire. Employees in the healthcare, building trades, shipping, energy management, or accounting, can be legally treated as *supervisors*. Any trade or skill can be affected, where the employees must direct others or exercise *independent judgments*, as part of doing their routine job. The bottom line is that the ruling has the potential to affect over 8 million employees, currently unionized or wishing to join unions. If a company can convert employees to *supervisor* status, the employer can effectively reduce the number of potential *employees* in the company, and reduce the union strength or influence at the workplace. It is a major blow to organized labor, and a significant victory for corporate America.

Organized Labor Political Activities

RESPECT Act

The Re-Empowerment of Skilled and Professional Employees and Construction and Trades-Workers Act, known as the RESPECT Act, is intended to undo the NLRB Kentucky River decisions defining *supervisors*. Representative Robert Andrews, (D-NJ), sponsor the bill, saying, *"The passage of the RESPECT Act will overturn the misguided decision of the NLRB in the Kentucky River trilogy and restore the law back to Congress' original intent. It will protect the right to organize and collectively bargain for millions of American workers."* (http://www.teamster.org/07news/hn_070921_1.asp).

Senator Chris Dodd (D-CT), Senators Richard Durbin (D-IL), and Edward Kennedy (D-MA), introduced the RESPECT Act in the Senate as companion legislation. The bill would remove the words *"assigned"* and *"responsibility to direct"* from the definitions of *"supervisors,"* and would require the worker to spend the majority of the day actually *"supervising."* *"The RESPECT Act is a critical and commonsense step to help protect workers' rights,"* said Dodd. *"Allowing employers to deny workers the right to unionize because their tasks require occasional and minor supervisory duties is unjust and frankly un-American. It is our responsibility to ensure that these hard-working individuals are treated fairly by their employers."* (http://dodd.senate.gov/index.php?q=node/3796).

This is an example of organized labors lobbying strength and the political power. Political parties support union issues with legislation. The political parties get strong union support, and the unions get strong pro labor legislation.

Employee Free Choice Act (EFCA)

The National Labor Relations Act, for the past 70 years, has recognized a labor union as the official bargaining agent representing employees only <u>after</u> the union wins a secret ballot election. The Employee Free Choice Act (EFCA), universally supported by organized labor, and sponsored by the Democratic Party, would require an employer to recognize a union <u>after</u> the authorization cards are signed (known as *Card Check*) by a simple majority (that is 50% plus 1) of the eligible workers.

The process would reduce the influence and control of labor consultants, and would create an easier, less costly and less contentious method than the current NLRB secret ballot election. Companies remain union free and defeat a union organizing campaign in greater numbers, after hiring labor consultants, and employing anti union organizing methods.

The EFCA would drastically improve organized labors chances of recognition, and thus would increase the number of unionized workers. This is a great help to organized labor, whose numbers, influence, and saturation have been rapidly declining for decades. Pro-employer groups, and anti-union organizations, with support from the Republican Party, have fought hard against the EFCA, because it would create faster and easier methods for unions to win. Corporate America wants less union interference, and unions want more influence in corporate America.

The Employee Free Choice Act, if enacted as organized labor wishes, would provide injunctions for specified Unfair Labor Practices (known as ULP's), during organizing drives and prior to union certification. When the NLRB certified the union, the parties would have 90 days to come to acceptable first contract terms, after which either party could ask the Federal Mediation and Conciliation Service (FMCS) to mediate the differences. If mediation fails after 30 days, the contract would be referred for binding arbitration. The decision of the arbitrator is final and a two-year contract is binding on all parties. The EFCA provide damages equal to twice-back pay, if the company violated certain Unfair Labor Practices, after recognition as the bargaining agent.

There are other civil penalties attached to the bill, designed to force employers to sign an acceptable first contract and to reduce intimidation and retribution for workers involved in unionizing attempts. For example:

> Civil Penalties: Provides for civil fines of up to $20,000 per violation against employers, who have been found to willfully or repeatedly violate the rights employees during an organizing campaign or first contract drive.
>
> Treble Back Pay: Increases the amount an employer

is required to pay when an employee is discharged or discriminated against during an organizing campaign or first contract drive to three times back pay.

Mandatory Applications for Injunctions: The NLRB must seek a federal court injunction against an employer whenever there is reasonable cause to believe the employer has discharged or discriminated against employees, threatened to discharge or discriminate against employees or engaged in conduct that significantly interferes with employee rights during an organizing or first contract drive. It authorizes the courts to grant temporary restraining orders or other appropriate injunctive relief. (www.employeefreechoiceact.org).

Organized labor maintains that the current organizing system is distorted in favor of business. U.S. labor laws are intended to protect workers rights to form unions. Labor unions express the opinion that in reality workers can risk losing their jobs to form a union. Employers, and labor consultants hired to fight unionization, use the NLRB to their advantage, when confronted with an organizing drive. Labor unions argue that employers routinely intimidate, harass, and fire workers as part of employers anti union strategy. The tactics used by labor consultants on occasion are persuasive, but the consequences are small compared to the advantages of keeping the union from winning. Kate Bronfenbrenner, Cornel University labor scholar, provided these observations involving organizing campaigns:

- *Ninety-two percent of private-sector employers, when faced with employees who want to join union, force employees to attend closed-door meetings to hear anti-union propaganda.*
- *Eighty percent require supervisors to attend training ses-*

sions on attacking union.
- *Seventy-eight percent require supervisors deliver anti-union messages to workers.*
- *Seventy-five percent hire outside consultants to run anti-union campaigns.*
- *Fifty percent of employers threaten to shut down ... if employees join a union.*
- *Twenty-five percent of organizing campaigns, private-sector employers illegally fire workers because they want to form a union.*
- *Thirty-three percent of employers do not negotiate a first contract.*

(http://www.aflcio.org/joinaunion/voiceatwork/efca/broken-system.cfm)

The EFCA, introduced in 2003, but failed to gain support. In 2005, Senator Ted Kennedy (D-MA) and Representative George Miller (D-CA) sponsored the bipartisan legislation in Congress. Organized labor has been lobbying for reforms to the traditional NLRB organizing methods, arguing that companies and management intimidate workers to vote against the union during organizing drives. Opponents of the legislation argue that employees will not be able to make informed decisions, because they will only hear the unions' side. Corporate America argues they will not be aware of an organizing drive until <u>after</u> the union has collected the required authorization cards, through the card check process.

Republican Vice President Dick Cheney told the National Association of Manufacturers on February 14, 2007 that the Bush White House "...would veto the bill... and opposes any effort to circumvent supervised elections and private balloting." (http://www.reference.com/search?q=employee%20free%20choice%20act#all). The Chamber of Commerce and various employer groups oppose the EFCA. Former Labor Secretary Elaine Chao, argued, "... worker's right to a secret ballot election is an intrinsic right ... that should not be legislated away at the behest of special interest groups." (http://www.jacksonlewis.com/legalupdates/article.cfm?aid=1073).

On February 14, 2007, in a full Committee markup session, the House Committee on Education and Labor voted 26-19 to report the bill to the full House. Republican members of the committee voted unanimously against reporting the bill, citing Republican amendments rejected by the Democratic majority on the committee.

On March 1, 2007, the House of Representatives passed the bill, by 241 - 185. Senator Edward Kennedy (D-MA), Chairman of the Senate Committee on Health, Employment, Labor, and Pensions, on March 30, 2007, introduced the Senate version of the Employee Free Choice Act.

The Senate on June 26, 2007 voted 51-48 on a *Motion to Invoke Cloture on the Motion to Proceed to Consider H.R. 800* (the House version). Because 60 votes were needed to invoke cloture (closure), the EFCA did not pass during the 110th Congress. (http://www.reference.com/search?q=employee%20free%20 choice%20act#all).

President Obama won the 2008 election and the Democratic Party may have the 6o votes needed for the EFCA to pass the 111 Congress. It is widely believed that some version of the Employee Free Choice Act may become law in 2009.

Most Democrats and a few Republicans support the Employee Free Choice Act. The highest support is among Democrats (83 %), followed by Midwesterners, and College Educated (74 % each), Southerners (65 %), Right-to-work states (65 %), Independents (63 %), and Republicans (54 %). (www.employeefreechoiceact.org).

EFCA is a current example of labor unions political strength, and is the top legislative priority for organized labor under the Obama administration. It is a crucial piece of pro-labor legislation, and if enacted as unions want, will help the labor movement regain the strength in numbers, and the political power it once had. The AFL-CIO, Change to Win, and the labor movement, have combined to flex their political and lobbying muscle to push this bill. The Democratic Party needs to win the allegiance and support of labor unions. Labor unions need to win pro labor legislation, to prove to their membership that they are viable and still have the political muscle to enhance the lives of their members.

Immigration and Labor Unions

The United States is a nation of immigrants, and immigrants helped build the nation. History has not been kind to those who left their home countries and chose to make America their home. Immigrants have been and still are exploited, treated poorly, and robbed of their dignity. In spite of all their hardships, this country could not have developed and prospered without the millions of immigrants who contributed their skills, knowledge, and culture. America is said to be a melting pot, but this author prefers to think of America as a large salad bowl. Each immigrant group brings its own culture, and adds their special flavors to the salad bowl. Each culture contributes to the final product.

Organized labor was skeptical of immigrants, fearing that collectively, they would bid down the cost of labor. If a particular immigrant or ethnic group were willing to work harder, for lower wages, in the factories or the fields, than another group or native born, then wages in that industry would be lower. Managers could bid out the work to those willing and able to worker harder for less. To an extent, this has become reality. Unions shunned immigrants and did not embrace their numbers. Immigrant workers by necessity, education, or skills, historically have chosen work that others do not want.

However, the tides of organized labor are changing. Unions are losing members, and consequently revenue and political power. Organizing new members is the key to growth, and growth is the key to union survival. A large segment of the population that has been largely ignored by labor unions has been immigrants, and collectively these workers need unionization, because they are underpaid, repressed, and exploited.

A few forward-looking labor organizations have seized this opportunity. These unions represent workers in low wage industries, such as office cleaners, hospitality workers, laundry workers and the like. Justice for Janitors, for example, has organized office cleaners and janitorial workers in Los Angeles and other large cities. UNITE represents needle trades workers such as those employed in the garment making industry. HERE represents hotel, and restaurant workers. The two unions combined to become UNITE-HERE and thus increase their membership and strength. SEIU represents various other low paid and low skilled office cleaners, maintenance, and industrial workers. Together, as a segment of the labor union industry, these unions represent millions of workers, are a formidable political block, and negotiate strong contracts with employers. A large portion of their membership base is first or second generation immigrants. Legacy labor unions, fearing a greater loss of membership in decaying industries, have also accepted that immigrants are a segment of the working population that offers hope in large numbers, because it is not saturated. This is growth market for organized labor.

The United Food and Commercial Workers Union (UFCW), which represents 1.4 million workers in the food industry, such as grocery store workers, and meat packers, are aggressively recruiting immigrant workers because they are a significant portion of the workforce. The UFCW has been organizing immigrant workers in the meatpacking industry since the 1970's. *"We are bringing a message of hope to immigrant workers. The workers who are doing America's work— the hard work— the dangerous work— the work that puts food on the dinner table for America's families. We believe that if you do the work, you've earned the opportunity for legal status, a living wage, and respect for your* rights. We are calling on America to recognize the contribution of some its most valuable workers," said UFCW President Doug Dority. (Immigrant Workers Put Food on the Table. Hispanic PR Wire. www.ufcw.org).

Upton Sinclair's novel <u>The Jungle</u>, spoke about the horrible conditions immigrant workers from Central and Southern Europe endured working in the meatpacking industry a century ago. Modern day immigrant workers from Southeast Asia, Latin America, and Africa are working in non-union meatpacking houses, with high injury rates and for low wages. The companies are exploiting the immigrants and threatening workers with deportation if they try to form a union. "*Employers ruthlessly exploit immigrant workers, who often have no understanding of workplace rights and who live in constant fear of deportation, and allowing employers' to threaten INS enforcement action against them. To protect American workplace standards, we must legalize and organize immigrant workers to stop the widespread abuse of worker rights,*" Dority said. (Immigrant Workers Put Food on the Table. Hispanic PR Wire. www.ufcw.org).

The UFCW contracts call for multi cultural training and bilingual safety classes, to protect workers from management abuses, such as illegal firings of immigrant workers, discrimination, to provide representation and arbitration, and to protect workers rights. Smithfield Foods in Tar Heel, North Carolina, for example, has hired labor consultants, or union busters, to prevent unions from winning organizing campaigns. A North Carolina jury found Smithfield Foods violated civil rights laws and an administrative law judge found widespread labor law violations. UFCW President Doug Dority said, "*…Every worker has an interest in stopping the exploitation of immigrant workers. If employers can get away violating the rights of any worker, they will be able to exploit all workers. Immigrant workers are the victims in a system that wants their labor, but at the same time deny them the rights and rewards of their work. That is not the American way!* (Immigrant Workers

Put Food on the Table. Hispanic PR Wire. www.ufcw.org).

Labor unions view immigrant workers as an untapped pool of workers who are potential union members. These groups of workers, from labor unions perspective, are in need of union representation and protection, because companies exploit them. Companies create the need for unions. Unhappy and exploited workers seek unionization for protection and collective representation. Happy workers usually do not seek union protection. The AFL-CIO supports strong protections for immigrant workers, as noted in the policy statement from the Executive Council. *"The current system of immigration enforcement is broken and needs to be reformed to allow undocumented workers to work lawfully in the United States, thus taking away employers' ability to exploit them based on their undocumented status. Future workers should come to this country with full rights, not as temporary workers. Immigration laws should be enforced in a manner that complements labor law enforcement. Raids and employer sanctions are powerful tools that employers have to diminish workers' rights."* (Our Immigration System is Broken, by James Parks. http://blog.aflcio.org/2007/04/08/our-immigration-system-is-broken/).

Immigration by the Numbers

The U.S. Census Bureau in 2003 noted that 33.7 million people are living in the U.S. are foreign born. This represents 12 % of the total population and 14% of the total civilian workers. There were 17.7 million foreign-born workers, and 104.7 million native workers in the United States, in 2003. The number of foreign-born union members has increased, and the number of native workers has decreased since 1996.

- 11% of foreign-born workers are union members or union

represented.
- 14.8% of native workers are represented by unions. More native workers than foreign-born workers are union represented.
- 24% increased in foreign-born union members from 1996 to 2003. The number of working immigrants represented by union increased 23% from 1996 to 2003.
- 6% decline in native union membership from 1996 to 2003.
- 12% of immigrants were union members in 1996 compared to 10% in 2003.
- 15% of natives were union members in 1996 compared to 13% in 2003.
- 2% increased in immigrant union members from 1996 to 2003.
- 48% increase in the total number of immigrant workers from 1996 to 2003. (http://www.migrationpolicy.org/pubs/7_Immigrant_Union_Membership.pdf.).

The dilemma faced by organized labor is, if unions seek immigration restriction, it alienates the very group that unions need to organize. If unions welcome immigrants, it inflates the labor supply and thus reduces labors ability to win high labor rate contracts. If unions support liberal immigration policies, non-union American workers would compete with immigrant workers for jobs, and the outcome would be to lower wages. Historically, union membership rates increased and decreased inversely to immigration rates. When union rates increased, immigration decreased, and when immigration increased, union rates decreased. (http://www.cis.org/articles/2001/back1001.html).

In the 1990's union membership was declining rapidly, and immigration was increasing dramatically. In 2000, the AFL-CIO Executive Council reversed itself, from anti-immigration, to fully supporting expanding immigration, declaring *"championing immigrant rights as a strategic move to make immigrants more enthusiastic about joining unions."* (http://www.cis.org/articles/2001/back1001.html). The reality is both unions and immigrants need each other. Unions need to organize immigrant workers to increase the declining union membership rates. Immigrant workers need unions to win better working conditions through collective bargaining, and for legal and political support.

When organized labor is trying to unionize a specific work place, unions are required to organize <u>all</u> the qualified workers hired by the employer. If the employer chooses to hire immigrant workers, either legal or illegal, and the union is organizing the work site, the union must include <u>all</u> the workers as part of the collective bargaining. To do otherwise is discrimination, and therefore illegal. For example, the union cannot say it will only organize and represent, the legal immigrant dockworkers, but will not organize or represent the illegal immigrant dockworkers. The union can choose to organize only the warehouse workers, and not the dockworkers, for example. However, the union must agree to represent all the warehouse workers equally, regardless of their immigration status. If the union does not wish to organize all the immigrants equally, the union cannot organize or represent <u>any</u> of the workers, and management will then seek to hire more non-union legal or illegal immigrant workers. Historically, unions have organized <u>all</u> the workers at the worksite, based on the need for collective representation to enhance their economic well-being. Therefore, it is a pragmatic decision to endorse immigration, and not necessarily a social, ethical, or moral decision.

NAFTA

The North American Free Trade Agreement or NAFTA, are various tri-lateral free trade agreements between the United States, Mexico, and Canada, that took effect in January 1994. The business model was to eliminate trade tariffs, and reduce investment restrictions between the three nations over a fifteen-year period. NAFTA has been very controversial, with ardent anti and pro supporters. Opponents argued NAFTA is not actually *free trade* but *government managed trade*. The World Bank has various studies, generally support NAFTA and related side agreements, as being positive and helping Mexico reduce its poverty rates. Tilateral trade has increased in the first ten years of NAFTA, and "... in the period of 1993–2004, total trade between the United States and its NAFTA partners increased 129.3%, 110.1% with Canada, and 100.9% with Mexico." (http://www.reference.com/search?q=nafta).

Maquiladoras are factories established in Mexico, that turn raw materials into manufactured goods for export to the U.S., Canada or internationally. This has become the basis of Mexican trade, and "...real income in the Maquiladoras sector has increased 15.5% since the implementation of NAFTA. The auto parts trade is the most important and represents 20% of total NAFTA trade." (http://www.reference.com/search?q=nafta).

Essentially, unions view NAFTA as anti-labor because it is a method for industry to produce products cheaper in Mexico, using non-union workers, and export to the U.S., Canada, and internationally, with little tariff restrictions. The manufacturers benefit by making products in low wage nations with abundant resources, no unions, and very little environmental restrictions. Unions lose well paying U.S. union jobs to Mexico, and companies benefit with higher profits, and little restrictions.

NAFTA Super Highway

The United States is developing plans to build a private super highway from the Mexican border, starting in Laredo, Texas and entering Canada from Duluth, Minnesota. The NAFTA Super Highway, when completed, will be a ten lane limited access super highway, as wide as four football fields, connecting Mexico and Canada, and running through the central United States.

As part of the international transportation system, passenger and freight rail lines will parallel the highway, and underground pipelines will carry oil, water, natural gas, electricity, and communications. The objective is to connect Mexico, the United States, and Canada into a seamless transportation system. The first leg of this international freight transportation system, the Trans Texas Corridor System (TTC-35), is scheduled to start construction in 2008.

Estimates for the completed 4,000-mile system are $183.5 billion, and will require purchasing 584,000 acres. Sections will be built and developed, as needed, over the next 50 years. The international road will be partially financed using private investors, who will operate the system as a privately operated toll road, and charge fees for the high-speed rail service, underground pipelines, and communications systems. Funding for the Trans-Texas Corridor was awarded to Cintra-Zachry. Cintra, S.A. is a Spanish international transportation development company (http://www.cintra.es/) and an international operator of 23 toll highways and car parking in 142 cities worldwide. Zachry Construction Corporation is a privately owned Texas construction and industrial maintenance company (http://www.zachry.com/about_overview.htm). The financial plan shows that bank loans or tax-exempt bonds will fund 78% of the cost, while 22% will be equity funded. *"Cintra-Zachry expects to have 12% returns on investment for their equity partners, after taxes, which equates to 16% return before taxes. The plan calls for paying off the bank loans and the bonds prior to retiring the equity... Cintra-Zachry expects to collect $114 billion in toll revenue. The usual bond financing has a 3:1 ratio between total fees collected and value of capital infrastructure. ... With TTC-35, the ratio is 13:1. Cintra-Zachry expects to collect $114 billion in tolls... The ... Texas State Auditor estimated the toll to be collected will be $104 billion or more."* (http://www.

reference.com/browse/wiki/Trans-Texas_Corridor)

International freight will enter the United States through Mexico, thus avoiding the Longshoreman's Union. The freight will be transported through the United States and Canada, using Mexican owned trucks, operated by Mexican drivers, and therefore circumventing the Teamsters Union. Organized labor views this business model as a major threat to traditional union territories, because it is virtually impossible to unionize. Global freight will be loaded in Mexican non-union freight facilities, and transported by non-union Mexican owned and operated trucks, on an international self-contained semi-private highway within the United States. This is another example of globalization as a significant factor leading to the declining traditional organized labor business model.

The North America Super Corridor Coalition, Inc., (NASCO) a non profit organization promoting the Super Highway says the system should be considered the "... *world's first international, integrated and secure, multi-modal transportation system along the International Mid-Continent Trade and Transportation Corridor to improve both the trade competitiveness and quality of life in North America."* (http://www.humanevents.com/article.php?id=15497).

Kansas City will be the central connection hub for the NAFTA Super Highway, and the first inland port and customs checkpoint. The Kansas City Smart Port, Inc. will operate the facility, which is an *"investor based organization supported by the public and private sector"* (http://www.humanevents.com/article.php?id=15497). The goals of the Kansas City Smart Port are "... *to grow the area's transportation industry by attracting businesses with significant transportation and logistics elements... and to make it cheaper, faster, more efficient, and secure for companies to move goods into, from, and through the Kansas City area* (http://www.kcsmartport.com/sec_about/about.htm).

From this location, international freight can be transported East, West, and points in between, reducing ground transportation time, and bypassing the major unionized freight handling facilities in Los Angeles and Long Beach, California. Freight handling, traditionally has been controlled by the International Longshoremen Union and related labor unions, and the International Brotherhood of Teamsters and related labor unions has usually controlled ground transportation, such as local and interstate trucking. Kansas and Texas are part of the 22 states known as "Right-to-Work" states, *"which prohibit unions from making membership or payment of dues or fees a condition of employment, either before or after hire."* (http://www.reference.com/browse/wiki/Right-to-work_law).

Mexican Trucks on U.S. Highways

An element of the NAFTA agreements, the Department of Transportation (DOT) has granted permission, part of a test program, for 100 Mexican trucking companies to have free access in the U.S., and Mexico has granted permission for 100 American trucking companies to travel freely in Mexico. Previously, Mexican trucks could only travel a short distance to distribution zones within the United States, where they unloaded their cargo, and returned to Mexico. The cargo is transferred on U.S. trucks to travel to their final destinations within the U.S. Canadian trucking companies have enjoyed free access to U.S. destinations, but not Mexican trucking companies. The U.S. Federal Motor Carrier Safety Administration, which regulates truck safety and driver requirements, says the Mexican vehicles and drivers must meet the same U.S. trucking safety standards.

The International Brotherhood of Teamsters (IBT) position is that allowing Mexican trucks on U.S. highways hurts American workers and compromises U.S. security. The real issue for the Teamsters is the loss of unionized jobs. The Teamsters have significant control and influence in the transportation, and trucking industry. This is a prime example of globalization affecting American workers on American soil.

IS ORGANIZED LABOR A DECAYING BUSINESS MODEL?

The Senate voted 74 to 24 to block Mexican trucks on U.S. roads. The Teamsters union still has strong political power. Political parties and candidates need the support of labor unions, and supporting blocking of Mexican trucks was an important political move and a strong economic necessity for the Teamsters and for organized labor.

The point is that organized labor, though severely weakened and in a downward spiral, still has strong political and economic influence. This is a small example of the Teamsters union ability to convince the Senate to temporarily stop Mexican trucks from transporting NAFTA goods on American roads.

CHAPTER 8

Conclusion

Is Organized Labor a Decaying Business Model? The answer is not a definitive yes <u>or</u> no, but rather yes <u>and</u> no. If organized labor continues in the same manner it has for the last century, then the probability of relevant existence in the next century is slim, and labor may become the one-century wonder. The economic forces of globalization are a major contributor to this evolution, as is the shift towards an internet based information society. The traditional blue-collar labor business model is being replaced with robotics, technology, outsourcing, downsizing, and globalization.

Organized labor is a huge industry, but still stuck in the last century and has failed to accept that the nature of work has changed. Business as usual, usually means that you are out of business. Market forces are forcing economic changes, and unless labor adapts quickly, it may become irrelevant in the global market. Virtually every product and most major services, can be performed totally or partially in low wage countries, or outsourced to lower wage states, using eager low-wage non-union workers.

The internet and technology, has created the global 24-hour

workday. When it is night in the west, it is day in the east and workers can perform back office functions ready for the next business day. Telephone communications is seamlessly transferring calls to worldwide call centers, where cheerful representatives, will answer your concerns in the language you have chosen. *"For English, press one, for Spanish, press two, and for other languages, press three,"* is the globalized method for customer service and business communications.

American car companies can make cars in China, and sell them in Detroit, cheaper than making the cars in Detroit, and selling them in America. These same American car companies can make cars in China and sell them worldwide, even cheaper, and for a greater profit, than selling the same cars in the United States. To an extent, labor unions are to blame. They have priced labor above economic returns. This oversight or greed is a significant contributor to the decline of the organized labor business model. Labor, in its basic element, is a commodity, like any raw material or production facility. Best business practices mandates that companies go where they make the most profit. Labor is expensive. Corporate America has fought back, by outsourcing, moving to non-union and less expensive environments, downsizing, embracing technology, and by aggressively fighting union organizing campaigns. It is not personal, just business.

The survival business model for organized labor is to become more relevant with the times and re-format itself to meet the needs of its members. Corporate America uses a similar model, as they shed old products, old production methods, and old marketing tools. In its place, corporate America emerges leaner and more agile, able to meet product demands quickly and adjust to market realities. Unions need to adjust their business model to market realities and become more membership centric and less fraternal.

Organized labor must look to the past to see the future. Labor unions have become complacent, unable, or unwilling to adjust to change. The axiom of unions being *'male, pale, and stale'* has merit. Unions are coming to the slow realization they must shed their old-boy ways, and embrace immigrants, minorities, service workers, and all disenfranchised workers. These are the under unionized and largely ignored growth sectors for unions. Traditional blue-collar workers in heavy industry are declining, and no company or industry wants to bet on a losing horse.

Politically and economically, the future for organized labor as an industry is with the sectors of the American economy that have been previously ignored. This includes service sector employment, low-wage workers, minorities, and immigrants. These disrespected workers desperately need the services that unions provide, which is protection from oppression, better wages, and benefits, better health care, and collective bargaining benefits, and they deserve respect and dignity. Unions must return to their roots. Historically, unions represented oppressed workers, which is exactly the category that immigrants, minorities, and low-wage workers represent.

Unions have seen better days. Private sector unions have experienced a rapid decline in saturation, as companies search for lower cost business models. Public sector unions are the bright spot, and these numbers are barely holding steady as governments on all levels are facing the dilemma of servicing more people with shrinking budgets.

The key to union growth, is organizing. The mantra *Organize or Perish* is an absolute. Organizing is the method for unions to grow their business. Companies expand by adding paying clients, and unions expand by adding dues paying members.

Corporate America wishes to remain non-union, and when faced with an organizing attempt, swings a heavy hammer spending vast sums to remain union free. The labor relations business (*union busting* in the labor vernacular) is a huge industry on to itself. This has been a contributing factor to the decline of unions. The goals of the labor relations consultants are to convince employees that unions are bad, and the company is good. Unions maintain that American labor laws are written to support the employer, and this makes organizing very difficult. Companies that hire professional labor consultants, have a significantly higher win rate over those companies that try to do it in house or do nothing at all. Unions thrive when employer and employee relationships are oppressive and exploitative. Unions have difficulties organizing companies when employees are happy, fairly compensated, and productive. Repressive employers create strong unions, and good companies do not have unions. Happy workers are productive workers and the employer and stakeholders all benefit.

Union labor has priced itself out of the global marketplace. Blue-collar industrial employment is outsourced to non-union low wage nations. Private industry must earn a profit or go out of business. "*Union Made in America*" is not an economic reality, given globalization and technology. Gone are the days of the *workers* versus *management* mentality. Labor must accept that to survive and prosper, they must become productive partners with business, not anti-productive adversaries. Welcome to the new reality.

The only slight stability is in the public sector. Organized labor contributes to political parties and campaigns, and therefore politicians do not want to bite the hand that feeds them, and placidly support government union organizing or remain neutral. Government services are not profit motivated and taxpayers support the increased labor costs. An unintended consequence of public sector unions is an entrenched bureaucracy where it is extremely difficult to terminate underperforming employees. The stereotype of lazy government workers is legendary, and when you compound the union job protection clauses, can become the perfect storm for incompetence. Unions tend to protect low productivity workers, support poor employee work ethics, and enable incompetency. The system rewards longevity and not productivity. The bureaucracy outlives the bureaucrats.

Foreign automakers (such as Honda and Toyota) are awarded tax incentives to build domestic factories, usually in lower wage states. The foreign automakers create blue-collar and white-collar jobs in states with high unemployment, low union saturation, and can improve the prevailing area wages. This raises the local standards of living, and improves the tax base, which in turn helps the local economy. It is a winning situation for all parties. The plants tend to be staffed with younger, non-union, less costly workers, and therefore the retirement and health care liabilities for the employers are less expensive. The legacy automakers are usually saddle with archaic union work rules, and staffed with unionized, older, higher paid workers, with expensive health care and retirement benefits.

If unions are to succeed and remain relevant, employers need to view workers and unions, not just as costs factors, but also as productive partners. A modern employer and progressive labor union, working together, and not as adversaries, can achieve higher productivity, and higher wages, with increased competitiveness and higher corporate profitability. A case in point is the comparison between Costco and Sam's Club (a Wal-Mart company). Both firms sell similar products to similar customers, and are aggressive competitors. Costco's labor costs are about 40% higher than Sam's Club is. In 2005, Costco's operating profit per employee was $21,805, as compared to Sam's Club of $11,615, and Costco's sales per square foot was $866, compared to $525 for Sam's Club. Moreover, Costco's employee turnover rate was only 6%, as compared to 21% for Sam's Club. Profit, productivity, and unionization can be positively related, if all partners work in concert. (Economic Policy Institute Briefing Paper. *Unions, the Economy, and the Employee Free Choice Act*. Briefing Paper #181. Shaiken, Harley. 2007).

One of the roles of government is to distribute economic prosperity to the workers who are both a major contributor and a major benefactor. Business and labor are mutually dependent on each other, and their success is based on a cooperative positive relationship. A company that fails to be profitable because of out dated and unrealistic labor policies, soon consolidates, files for bankruptcy or closes shop, and the workers loose. An empty factory or closed store does not need workers. Simply put, no employer, no employees!

The American Dream, and thus the nation's "_American Dream_" of economic prosperity are co-dependent on productive labor relations. Globalization, outsourcing, downsizing, technology, and the internet are real threats to the American blue-collar worker. "_Union Made in America_" has become a history lesson, and now might mean, at best, "_Maybe Partially Assembled in America._" A realistic economic alternative is a mutually dependent and respectful labor and management relationship, with government acting as a helpful *"consigliore"* or counselor and advisor to both sides.

Government plays a very active role in American prosperity, by establishing and developing economic initiatives, and labor policies that benefit workers, and support economic growth policies. Government needs to institute macroeconomic policies to support long-term job creation, and to provide the tools to educate, train and support workers and their families. Microeconomic policies, such as local job creation requires the sustained support of government, industry, and unions, to provide the education, training, and career paths to create jobs consistent with industry and community needs.

Foreign trade policies with low wage nations, may have led union and non-union American workers in an economic race to the bottom. Global labor standards and trade agreements, must protect workers, and eliminate all forms of child labor, compulsory labor, and other discriminatory labor practices. Sweatshops may produce cheap shirts for Wal-Mart, but not at the expense of women and children working for sub-poverty wages under inhuman conditions. It is morally wrong and economically short sighted.

From a macroeconomic perspective, these forms of global

CONCLUSION

trade practices do not produce long-term growth, and ultimately lead to a wage race to the bottom. Without enforceable trade policies, American workers will not be able to compete. Ultimately, workers in less developed countries will be hurt, and this will drive those nations' workers into deeper poverty, political and economic unrest, and severe desperation.

All workers need to earn a living wage, in order to support a family and to grow the economy. Workers at the lower end of the wage scale, require larger social services supports, and contribute little to the economic welfare of the nation as a whole. Raising the federal minimum wage to a level that may actually support a family is an example of a government policy that positively affects the family, and in the long term the nation. To keep up with the real purchasing power, wages must be higher than the federal minimum and relative to the local economy. Higher wages provide positive benefits to society and taxpayers, by increasing the families buying power, which stimulates production and consumption, and reduces dependency on social services and government programs.

Lifetime employment, if it ever really existed in the United States, is an outdated concept and does not connect with a fast changing global environment. Advances in technology and global competitive realities have reduced the power of the unionized rank-and-file worker, and add to the pressure of management to increase corporate profitability. This has fundamentally changed the nature of work. No longer does a unionized blue-collar or white-collar employee expect to spend their entire working lives with one employer, and retire with a gold watch and a small pension for a lifetime of service.

Employers have a talent war for the best workers they can afford, and the better employers create workplace cultures based on employee satisfaction and career development. Employees want to feel they are making a difference. The talent wars have created friendlier work environments, such as fitness and day care centers, helping families balance work and family time, offering time off to care for children or an elderly parent, and caring bosses willing to give workers flexible time schedules to reduce commuting stress. (http://tech.groups.yahoo.com/group/TechsUnite/message/25991).

The reality is the old ways of doing business do not work in the new global market place. Labor unions need to become a value added partner with business, not an adversary to economic survival. The *labor unions* versus *management* mindset will lead to labor without a place to work, because management has outsourced work, reduced production, merged, consolidated, or moved the industry to a lower cost environment. *"If unions are going to survive and prosper in the 21st century, we still need to meet the needs of workers, but we also need to find a way to serve important business needs… We can no longer simply demand that business adapt to our needs. We need to adapt to the needs of business…"* (http://www.virginiaclassifieds.com/biz/virginiabusiness/magazine/ yr2006/dec06/ideas.shtml).

Labor unions understand the needs of the workers, but few unions understand and accept the needs of business. This is a very important concept often ignored. When an employer does not earn a profit, the business will be out of business, and does not need workers. There are no winners, just looser. The business loses, the workers loose, and the communities loose.

The nature of work has changed, and unions must change together to meet global market demands. The key to long-term union survival, increased economic strength, and political power lies in the ability to adapt to changes. In other words, organized labor must become productive allies with business, and become part of the solution, not part of the problem. To do less will result in a decayed organized labor business model creating its own irrelevance, and labor unions will soon go the way of the dinosaurs.

"If organized labor continues to do what it has always done, it will continue to get less than it has always got."
-Anonymous-

Bibliography

AFL-CIO union (American Federation of Labor-Congress of Industrial Organizations). Web site www.aflcio.org.
Myths and Facts about Unions. Retrieved August 29, 2007, from http://www.aflcio.org/aboutunion.cfm
AFL-CIO Affiliate Per Capita Taxes. Retrieved September 02, 2007, from http://www.aflcio.org/aboutus/thisistheaflcio/ecouncil/ec08072007k.cfm and http://www.aflcio.org/aboutus/thisistheaflcio/constitution/art16.cfm
American Jobs: Going, Going... Retrieved July 12, 2007, from http://www.aflcio.org/aboutus/thisistheaflcio/publications/magazine/0903_amjobs.cfm.
Statement by AFL-CIO General Counsel Jon Hiatt on Supreme Court Decision Davenport v. Washington Education Association June 14, 2007. Retrieved September 21, 2007, from http://www.aflcio.org/mediacenter/prsptm/pr06142007.cfm
Employee Free Choice Act web site. Retrieved September 25, 2007, from www.employeefreechoiceact.org and www.aflcio.org/joinaunion/voiceatwork/efca/
The System for Forming Unions is Broken. Retrieved September 25, 2007, from http://www.aflcio.org/joinaunion/voiceatwork/efca/brokensystem.cfm

Our Immigration System is Broken, by James Parks. Retrieved October 1, 2007, from http://blog.aflcio.org/2007/04/08/our-immigration-system-is-broken/

Audience Dialogue. *What Is A Business Model?* Retrieved June 24, 2007 from http://www.audiencedialogue.org/busmod.html

Bond, Schoeneck & King, PLC, law firm. Web site www.bsk.com *Labor and Employment Law Information Memo: Weingarten Rights.* Retrieved July 28, 2007, from http://www.lawfirmalliance.com/assets/attachments/81.pdf

Burke Group, labor relations firm website. Retrieved September 11, 2007, from http://www.tbglabor.com

Business Model Design and Innovation.
Blog, What Is A Business Model? Retrieved June 24, 2007 from http://business-model-design.blogspot.com/2005/11/what-is-business model.html.

Career Builder job web site. Retrieved August 14, 2007, from www.careerbuilder.com.

Center for Immigration Studies. Web site www.cis.org
American Unionism and U.S. Immigration Policy. Retrieved July 1, 2007, from http://www.cis.org/articles/2001/back1001.html

Center for Responsive Politics. Open Secrets.Org. Web site www.opensecrets.org
Labor: Top Contributors to Federal Candidates and Parties. Retrieved September 19, 2007, from http://www.opensecrets.org/industries/contrib.asp?Ind=P&cycle=2006 http://www.opensecrets.org/industries/indus.asp?Ind=P

Center for Union Facts. Web site www.unionfacts.com.
Glossary of Terminology. Retrieved August 02, 2007, from http://www.unionfacts.com/glossary.cfm
Specific data for selected labor unions. Retrieved September

05, 2007, from http://www.unionfacts.com/unions/unionProfile.cfm?id=106
http://www.unionfacts.com/unions/unionFinances.cfm?id=93&year=2006
http://www.unionfacts.com/unions/unionFinances.cfm?id=106&year=2006
http://www.unionfacts.com/unions/unionProfile.cfm?id=289
http://www.unionfacts.com/unions/unionProfile.cfm?id=107
http://www.unionfacts.com/unions/unionFinances.cfm?id=511&year=2006
http://www.unionfacts.com/unions/unionProfile.cfm?id=511#UnfairLabor
http://www.unionfacts.com/unions/index.cfm
Use of Dues for Politics. Retrieved September 16, 2007, from http://www.unionfacts.com/articles/unionPolitics.cfm

Citizens for Limited Taxation & Government. Web site www.cltg.org *The "Beck" Decision and How it Affects You*. Retrieved September 18, 2007, from http://www.cltg.org/cltg/unions/howitaffectsyou.htm

Cintra Concesiones De Infraestructuras De Transporte, S.A. Web site http://www.cintra.es/index.asp

Corporate Campaign, Inc. *Spotlight on Union Busters by Tim Lally*. Retrieved, July 28, 2004, from http://www.corporatecampaign.org/lally.htm
http://www.corporatecampaign.org/bust2.htm
http://www.corporatecampaign.org/bust3.htm
http://www.corporatecampaign.org/bust4.htm
http://www.corporatecampaign.org/bust5.htm

Cool Fire Technology. *Brain Bank-Human Resources-National Labor Relations Board*. Retrieved July 28, 2007, from http://www.cftech.com/BrainBank/HUMANRESOURCES/NatlLabRelBd.html

Delaware News Journal. www.delawareonline.com.

Delaware Workers Sing Blue Collar Blues. Posted February 18, 2007. Retrieved August 09, 2007, from http://www.delawareonline.com/apps/pbcs.dll/article?AID=/20070218/BUSINES S/302180008/1003

Detroit News. Web site www.detnews.com
Autos Insider. Retrieved August 05, 2007, from http://www.detnews.com/2005/autosinsider/0510/17/A01-351179.htm
http://www.detnews.com/2005/autosinsider/0508/30/C01-297348.htm
http://www.detnews.com/2005/autosinsider/0505/04/A01-169975.htm
http://www.detnews.com/2005/autosinsider/0504/28/A01-162446.htm

Economic Policy Institute. Web site www.epinet.org
Supervisors in Name Only. Briefing Paper #225. Eisenbray, R and Michel, L. Retrieved September 19, 2007, from http://www.epinet.org/content.cfm/ib225
Unions, the Economy, and the Employee Free Choice Act. Briefing Paper #181. Shaiken, Harley. February 2007. Retrieved Sept 5, 2007, from http://www.epinet.org/content.cfm/ib181
A New Social Contract-Restoring Dignity and Balance to the Economy. Briefing Paper #184. Kochan, Thomas and Schulman, Beth. February 2007. Retrieved September 9, 2007, from http://www.epinet.org/content.cfm/ib184

Find Law for Legal Professionals. Web site www.findlaw.com
U.S. Supreme Court: NLRB v. Weingarten, Inc. 420 U.S. 251 (1975). Retrieved October 7, 2007, from http://caselaw.lp.findlaw.com/scripts/getcase.pl?court=us&vol=420&invol=251

Glossary of Political Economy Terms. Paul M. Johnson, Department of Political Science, Auburn University. Retrieved July 30, 2007 from http://www.auburn.edu/~johnspm/gloss/right-to-work

Hands On Network. www.handsonnetwork.org. *Why do US Companies Outsource Jobs? What Trends and Controversies Surround Outsourcing?* Retrieved August 4, 2007, from http://www.handsonnetwork.org/vca/employment-faqs/

Hoover Institution, Public Policy, Campaign Finance, Supreme Court Cases.
Web site www.campaignfinacesite.org
U.S. Supreme Court, Communications Workers v. Beck, 487 U.S. 735 (1988). Retrieved September 22, 2007, from http://www.campaignfinancesite.org/court/communication1.html

Human Events. Web site www.humanevents.com
Bush Administration Quietly Plans NAFTA Super Highway. Retrieved July 12, 2007, from http://www.humanevents.com/article.php?id=15497

Immigration and American Unionism, by Vernon M. Briggs, Jr. Ithaca, N.Y. Cornell University Press, 2001

Intellectual Ammunition Department of the Objectivist Newsletter. Retrieved July 21, 2007 from http://www.nathanielbranden.com/catalog/articles_essays/labor_unions.html

Intellectual Ammunition Department of the Objectivist Newsletter Planning for Freedom, 2nd ed., Libertarian Press, 1962, pp. 151-152

International Brotherhood of Electrical Workers (IBEW) union. Web site www.ibew.org.
Union Dues. Local 45, Hollywood, CA. Retrieved August 31, 2007, from http://ibew45.org/dues_benefits/dues_payment_info.html
A Guide to Basic Law and Procedures under the National Labor Relations Act. Retrieved September 13, 2007, from www.ibew.org/eworkers/legal/nlrb2.pdf

International Brotherhood of Teamsters (IBT) union. Web site www.teamster.org.

Job Bank. Retrieved September 03, 2007, from www.teamster.org/benefits/jobbank.htm
Airlines. Retrieved September 03, 2007, from www.teamster.org/divisions/airline/airline.asp
Public Services. Retrieved, September 04, 2007, from www.teamster.org/divisions/publicservices/publicservices.asp
Motion Pictures. Retrieved September 04, 2007, from www.teamster.org/divisions/motionpicture/mopicture.asp
The RESPECT Act: What it Means to You. Retrieved September 28, 2007, from http://www.teamster.org/07news/hn_070921_1.asp

Jackson Lewis, Inc., labor relations website. Retrieved, September 11, 2007, from http://jacksonlewis.com and http://www.jacksonlewis.com/legalupdates/article.cfm?aid=155 and
http://www.jacksonlewis.com/legalupdates/article.cfm?aid=598 and
http://www.jacksonlewis.com/legalupdates/article.cfm?aid=250
Employee Free Choice Act Reintroduced in Congress: The Battle Begins. Retrieved September 24, 2007, from http://www.jacksonlewis.com/legalupdates/article.cfm?aid=1073
Unionized Public Sector Employees Have No Right To Representation At Investigatory Interviews. Retrieved June 21, 2007, from http://www.jacksonlewis.com/legalupdates/article.cfm?aid=1075

Kansas City Smart Port, Inc. Web site www.kcsmartport.com
About Smart Port. Retrieved October 11, 2007, from http://www.kcsmartport.com/sec_about/about.htm

Kelber, H. (Ed.) (1997). *A Training Manual for Union Organizers*. New York: The Labor Educator.

Kelber, H. (Ed.) (2002). *A New Game Plan for Union Organizing*. New York: The Labor Educator.

Labor Notes. Web site www.labornotes.org.
Give Your Union a Dues Checkup. Brenner, Mark. Retrieved August 31, 2007, from http://www.labornotes.org/node/908.

Levitt, M.J. (1993). *Confessions of a Union Buster.* New York: Crown Publishers.

Mackinac Center for Public Policy. Web site, www.mackinac.org. *The Michigan Union Accountability Act: A Step Toward Accountability and Democracy in Labor Organizations.* Hunter, Robert and Kersey, Paul. Retrieved August 5, 2007, from http://www.mackinac.org/article.aspx?ID=3950.

Michigan Privatization Report. *Privatization Bears Fruit in the Big Apple.* Jahr, Michael. 2007. Retrieved August 10, 2007, from www.mackinac.org.
Communications Workers v. Beck. Retrieved September 13, 2007, from http://www.mackinac.org/article.aspx?ID=1401

Merriam Webster's Collegiate Dictionary, Tenth Edition, 1997.

Microsoft Encarta Online Encyclopedia. Web site www.encarta.msn.com.
Labor Union. Borjas, George. Retrieved September 01, 2007, from www.encarta.msn.com/text_761553112___0/Labor_Union.html

Migration Policy Institute. Web site www.migrationpolicy.org *Immigrant Union Members Numbers and Trends.* Retrieved July 30, 2007, from http://www.migrationpolicy.org/pubs/7_Immigrant_Union_Membership.pdf.

Migration Policy Institute Immigration Facts. Retrieved October 2, 2007, from www.migrationpolicy.org/pubs/fact_sheets.php

National Education Association (NEA). Web site www.nea.org. *Teacher Spending on Supplies and Union Dues.* Retrieved September 01, 2007, from http://educationchoice.blogspot.com/2006/11/teacher-spending-on-supplies- and-union.html

National Labor Relations Board pamphlet. *The National Labor Relations Board and You, Unfair Labor Practices.* Available from the Superintendent of Documents, U.S. Government Printing Office, Washington, DC 20402. Retrieved July 01, 2007, from http://www.nlrb.gov/nlrb/shared_files/brochures/engrep.asp

National Labor Relations Board. Web site www.nlrb.gov.

National Labor Relations Board's Case Activity Tracker (CATS) system.
Decertifying a Union. Retrieved September 12, 2007, from http://www.nlrb.gov/Workplace_Rights/i_am_new_to_this_website/how_do_i_file_a_petition_to_start_or_remove_a_union.aspx.
A Guide to Basic Law and Procedures under the National Labor Relations Act. Retrieved July 01, 2007, from http://library.findlaw.com/articles/00039/004851.pdf

National Legal and Policy Center. Web site. http://www.nlpc.org.

National Right to Work Legal Defense Foundation, Inc. Web site www.nrtw.org.
Retrieved July 29, 2007, from http://www.nrtw.org/rtws.htm
Big Labor's Massive Political Machine. Retrieved September 15, 2007, from http://www.nrtw.org/d/political_spending.htm

New Jersey Star-Ledger newspaper. *Manufacturing Smiles to Win Talent Wars,* by Beth Fitzgerald, Staff Reporter. June 24, 2007 Blog. Retrieved August 12, 2007, from http://tech.groups.yahoo.com/group/TechsUnite/message/25991
http://tech.groups.yahoo.com/group/TechsUnite/message/25991

New York Times. Web site www.nytimes.com
Your Money. Retrieved August 06, 2007, from http://www.nytimes.com/2007/02/25/business/yourmoney/25view.html?_r=1&ref=business&oref=slogin
and http://www.nytimes.com/2007/08/05/business/yourmoney/05homefront.html?ref=business

Osborne, David, and Gaebler, Ted. 1992. *Reinventing Government: How the Entrepreneurial Spirit is Transforming the Public Sector.* Reading, Mass.
Addison-Wesley Publishing Co., Inc. Retrieved August 23, 2007, from http://www.urban.org/publications/407023.html

People's Weekly World Newspaper Online. *Confessions of a Union Buster.* Retrieved September 13, 2007, from http://www.pww.org/article/articleprint/4255

Princeton University Industrial Relations. *Notes on the Economics of Labor Unions.*
Working Paper No. 452. Farber, Henry. Princeton University. 2001.

Princeton University Industrial Relations. *Non-Union Wages Rates and the Threat of Unionization.* Working Paper No. 472. Farber, Henry. Princeton University. 2003.

Princeton University Press. www.princeton.edu.
The Meaning of Privatization. Starr, Paul. Yale Law and Policy Review 1988. Retrieved August 23, 2007, from http://www.princeton.edu/~starr/meaning.html

Progressive Policy Institute. *Understanding the Offshoring Challenge.* Policy Report.
May 2004. Retrieved August 3, 2007, from www.ppionline.org

Power Through Information. Retrieved, September 11, 2007, from http://www.ptilaborresearch.com/home.html and http://www.ptilaborresearch.com/research_custom.html.

Power Through Information. Retrieved August 14, 2007, from http://www.ptilaborresearch.com/home.html

Public Administration and Management: An Interactive Journal. www.pamij.com
Downsizing and Organizational Culture. Hickok, Thomas. Retrieved August 16, 2007, from http://www.pamij.com/hickok.html

Reason Foundation. www.reason.org. *Transforming Government Through Privatization.*
Annual Privatization Report 2006. Retrieved August 22, 2007, from www.reason.org/privatization

Referrence.com. *Encyclopedia on Line.* Retrieved, July 03, 2007, from http://www.reference.com/browse/wiki/Right-to-work_law
http://www.reference.com/browse/wiki/Eight-hour_day
http://www.reference.com/search?q=AFL-CIO%20
http://www.reference.com/search?r=13&q=Congress%20of%20Industrial%20Org anizations
http://www.reference.com/search?q=change%20to%20win
http://www.reference.com/search?q=collective%20bargaining
http://www.reference.com/search?q=Labor%20contract
http://www.reference.com/search?q=right%20to%20work%20laws&r=d&dbweb
http://dictionary.reference.com/browse/privatization
The Employee Free Choice Act. Retrieved September 21, 2007, from http://www.reference.com/search?q=employee%20free%20choice%20act#all
North American Free Trade Agreement (NAFTA). Retrieved October 9, 2007, from http://www.reference.com/search?q=nafta
Trans-Texas Corridor. Retrieved October 13, 2007, from http://www.reference.com/browse/wiki/Trans-Texas_Corridor

Right-to-Work Laws. Retrieved October 11, 2007, from http://www.reference.com/browse/wiki/Right-to-work_law

Senator Chris Dodd-Democrat from Connecticut. Web site www.dodd.senate.gov
Dodd Introduces Legislation to Protect Workers' Right to Unionize. Retrieved September 27, 2007, from http://dodd.senate.gov/index.php?q=node/3796

Service Employees International Union-United Healthcare Workers (SEIU- UHW) union Web site www.seiu-uhw.org.

How much are Union Dues? Retrieved August 30, 2007, from www.seiu-uhw.org/organizing/union faqs.html#How_much_are_union_dues

Service Employees International Union (SEIU Local 1199) union. Web site www.1199SEIU.org.
How much are Union Dues? Retrieved August 30, 2007, from http://www.1199seiu.org/join/formingunion.cfm#Q6

SEIU Glossary of Union Terms. Retrieved September 04, 2007, from http://www.seiu.org/olc/workshop/glossary.html

Sheppard, Mullin, Richter, and Hampton, labor relations firm website. Retrieved September 13, 2007, from http://www.smrh.com, and http://www.smrh.com/practices-105.html

Sheppard, Mullin, Richter, and Hampton, labor relations. Retrieved August 14, 2007, from http://www.smrh.com

Smith Center for Private Enterprise Studies.
The Public and the Unions, by Charles W. Baird. Retrieved August 16, 2007, from http://www.sbe.csuhayward.edu/~sbesc/04marcol.html

Snell & Wilmer, L.L.P. The Workplace Word. Web site www.swlaw.com
Outsourcing and the Duty to Bargain. September 2004. Retrieved August 15, 2007 from www.swlaw.com

Social Studies Help Center web site. *The Labor Movement in America.* Retrieved June 22, 2007, from http://www.socialstudieshelp.com/Eco_Unionization.htm

Supreme Court of the Unites States. SCOTUS Blog. Web site www.scotusblog.com
More on the Decision of "Davenport v. WEA." Retrieved September 21, 2007, from http://www.scotusblog.com/movabletype/archives/2007/06/more_on_the_dec_2.html

Supreme Court of the United States. *Gary Davenport, et al v. Washington Education Association.* Nos. 05-1589 and 05-1657. Opinion of the Court, June 14, 2007.

Tom Paine Common Sense. Web site www.tompaine.com
Muzzling Unions by Dmitri Iglitzin. Retrieved September 11, 2007, from http://www.tompaine.com/articles/2007/01/22/muzzling_unions.php

United Food and Commercial Workers union. Web site. www.ufcw.org
What to Expect when Organizing a Union. Retrieved September 11, 2007, from http://www.ufcw.org/get_a_union/organizing_101/typical_campaign/index.cfm

United Food and Commercial Workers Union (UFCW). Web site www.ufcw.org
Immigrant Workers Put Food on the Table. Hispanic PR Wire. Retrieved July 8, 2007, from Hispanic PR Wire www.ufcw.org

Union Free America web site. *Union Free America.* Retrieved July 02, 2007, from
http://www.unionfreeamerica.com/duesforpolitics.htm
http://www.unionfreeamerica.com/union_membership.htm
http://www.unionfreeamerica.com/decertifying.htm
http://www.unionfreeamerica.com/union_corruption.htm
http://www.unionfreeamerica.com/duesforpolitics.htm

Unions Don't Spend Dues Dollars on Politics. Retrieved July 29, 2007, from http://www.unionfreeamerica.com/duesforpolitics.htm

Urban Institute. www.urban.org.
Privatization of Public Social Services. Nightingale, Demetra, and Pindus, Nancy.
Background Paper posted October 1997. Retrieved August 23, 2007, from http://www.urban.org/publications/407023.html

United States Department of Labor. Bureau of Labor Statistics. Web site www.bls.gov.
Bureau of Labor Statistics. Retrieved July 30, 2007 from web site: www.bls.gov.

Union Membership in 2006. USDL 07-0113 News Release. Retrieved September 01, 2007, from http://www.bls.gov/news.release/union2.nr0.htm

Bureau of Labor Statistics. *Employee Benefits in Private Industry, 2000.*

United States Department of State. Web site www.usinfo.state.gov. Outline of the United States Economy. *Labor in America: The Worker's Role.* Retrieved June 21, 2007, from http://usinfo.state.gov/products/pubs/oecon/chap9.htm

United Steel Workers union. Web site www.usw.org. Retrieved June 29, 2007, from http://www.usw.org/usw/program/content/291.php

UnionWeb.org web site. *A Short History of American Labor.* Original text appeared from American Federationist, March 1981. Retrieved June 27, 2007, from http://www.albany.edu/history/history316/LaborMovementHistory1.html

Virginia Business Magazine. *Labor Unions Need to Understand Business Issues,* by Denise Martire for Virginia Business, 2004. Retrieved August 16, 2007 from http://www.virginiaclassifieds.com/biz/virginiabusiness/magazine/yr2006/dec06/ ideas.shtml

Virginia Tech University, Center for Public Administration and Policy. www.cpap.vt.edu
Labor Union Bargaining-Trends In A Global Economy, by Harold Pitts, April 15, 2007. Retrieved August 19, 2007 from http://www.cpap.vt.edu/HighTable_2007/docs/Harold%20Pitts.doc

Wikipedia. Web site www.wikipedia.org.
The Business Model. Retrieved June 24, 2007 from http://en.wikipedia.org/wiki/Business_model
http://www.reference.com/search?q=labor%20unions

Working Life Blog. Web site www.workinglife.org
Kentucky River: Bad News. Retrieved September 22, 2007, from http://workinglife.typepad.com/daily_blog/2006/10/kentucky_river_.html

Workers Online. *Review: 2000-Issue 67: Confessions of a Union Buster.* Retrieved September 12, 2007, from http://workers.labor.net.au/67/d_review_costa.html

World Book Dictionary, 1977.

Ziff Davis, CIO Insight. www.cioinsight.com. *Unions Step Up Organizing of IT Workers, Outsourcing Fight.* September 2005. Retrieved August 12, 2007, from http://www.cioinsight.com/print_article2/0,1217,a=159450,00.asp

Zachry Construction Corporation. Web site www.zachry.com. Company Overview. Retrieved October 13, 2007, fromhttp://www.zachry.com/about_overview.htm